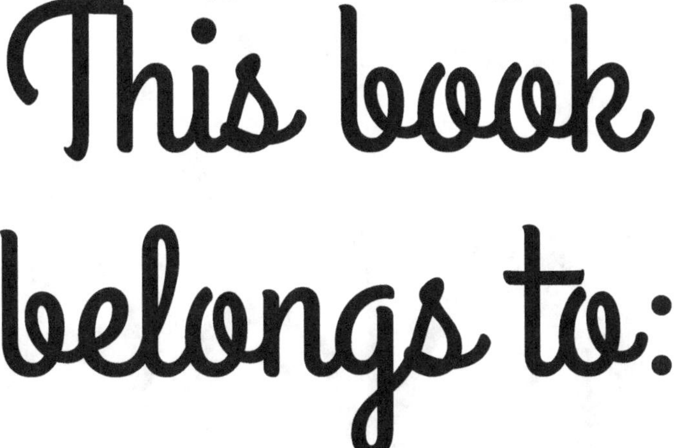

This book
belongs to:

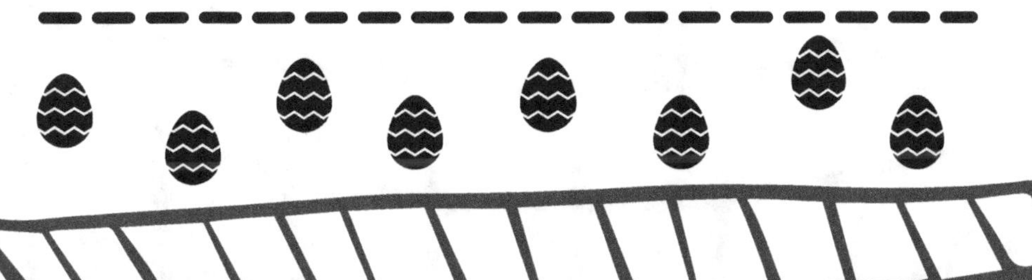

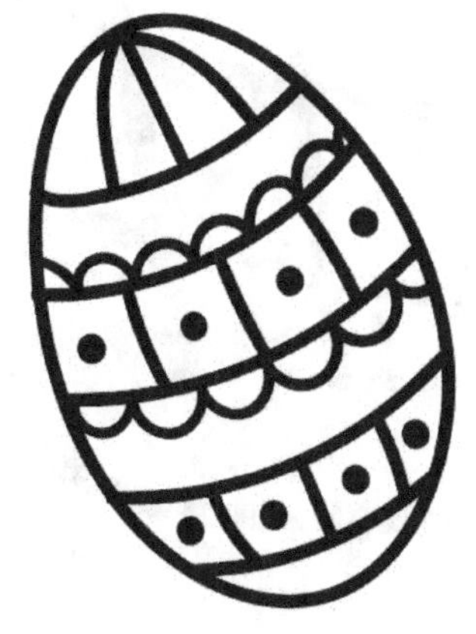

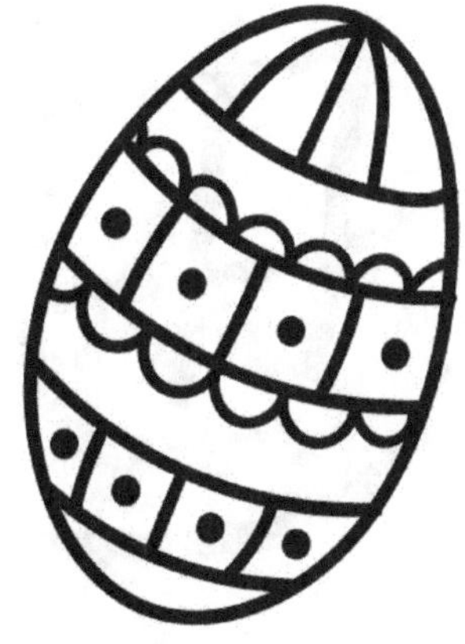

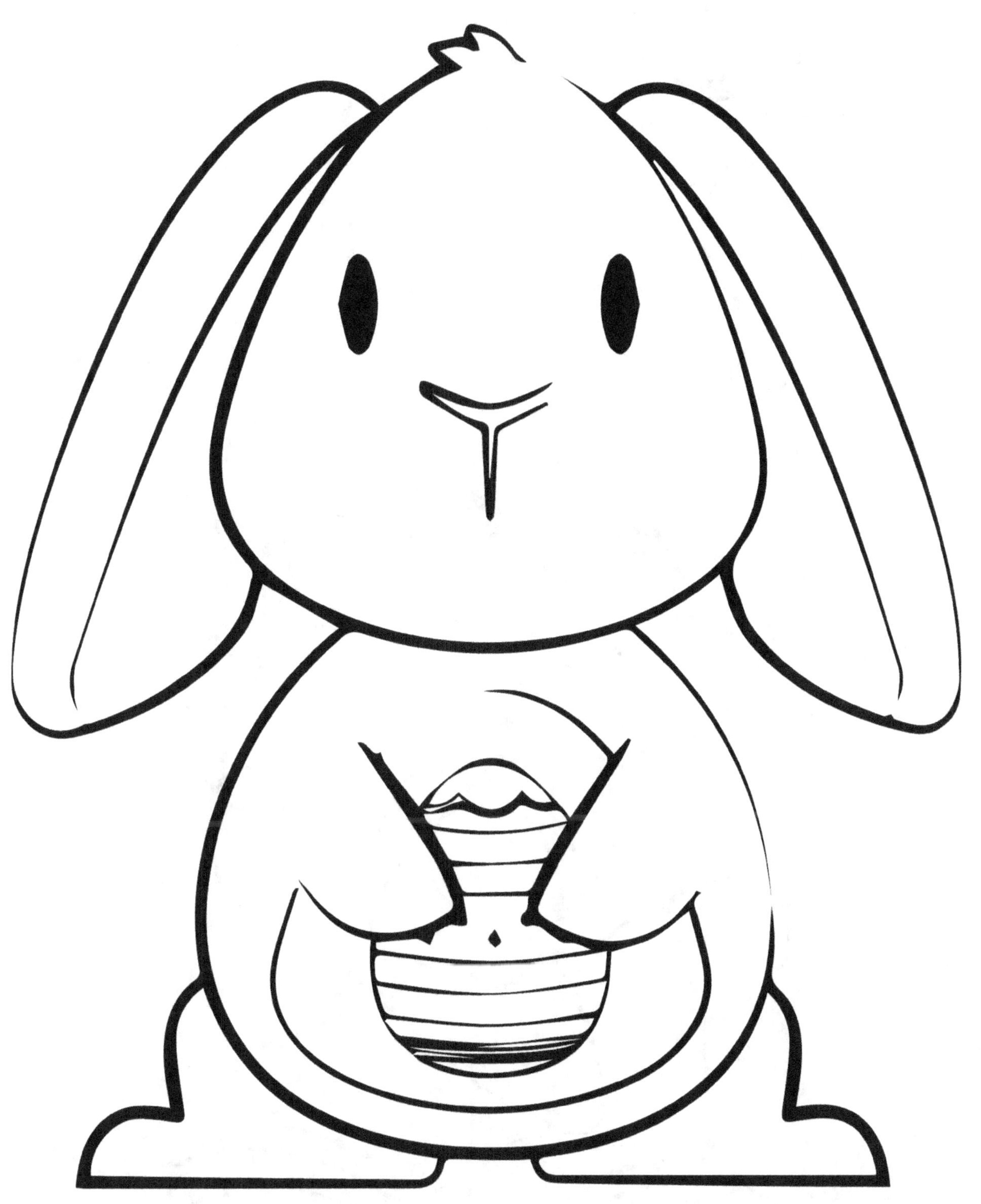

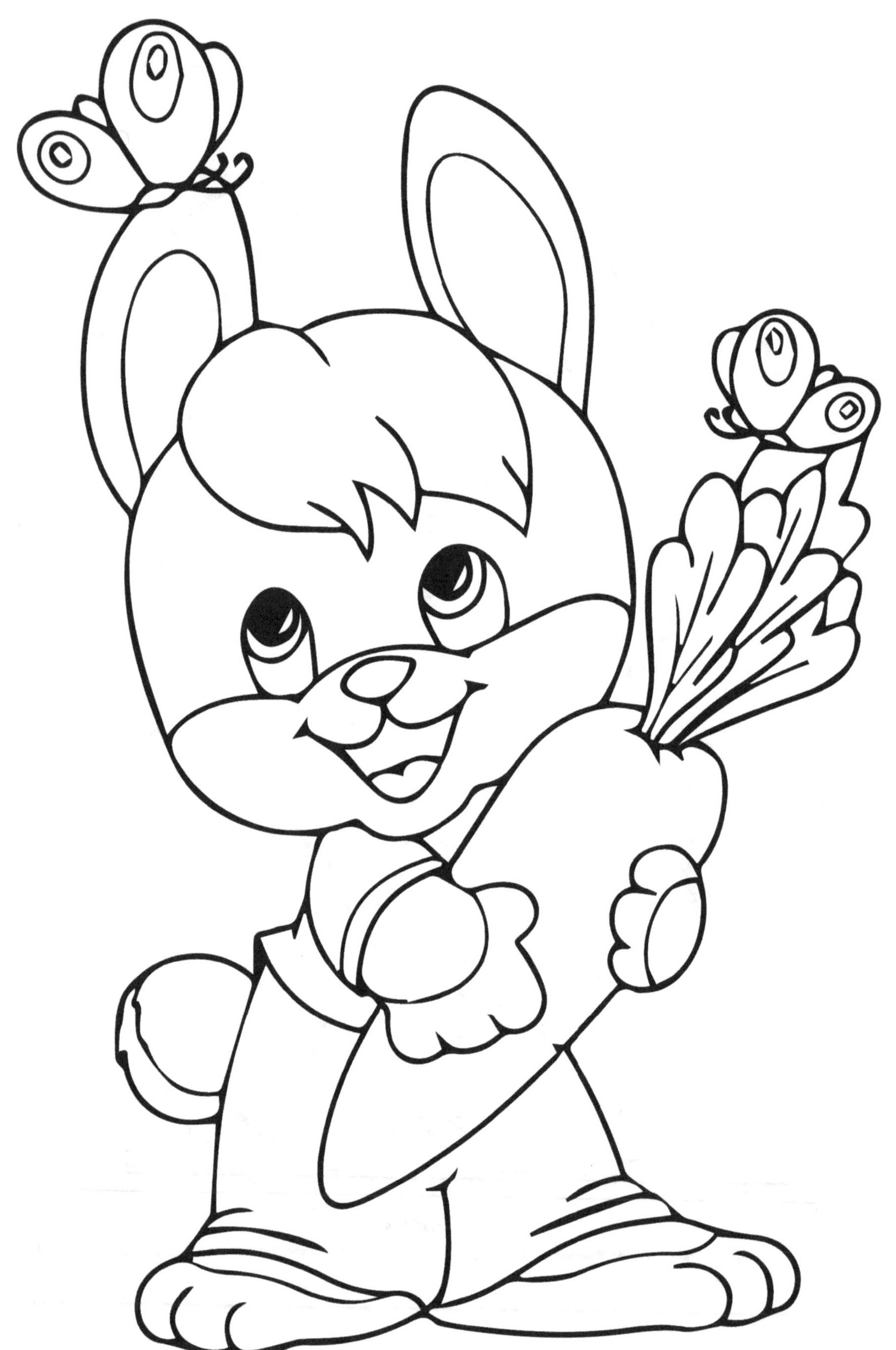

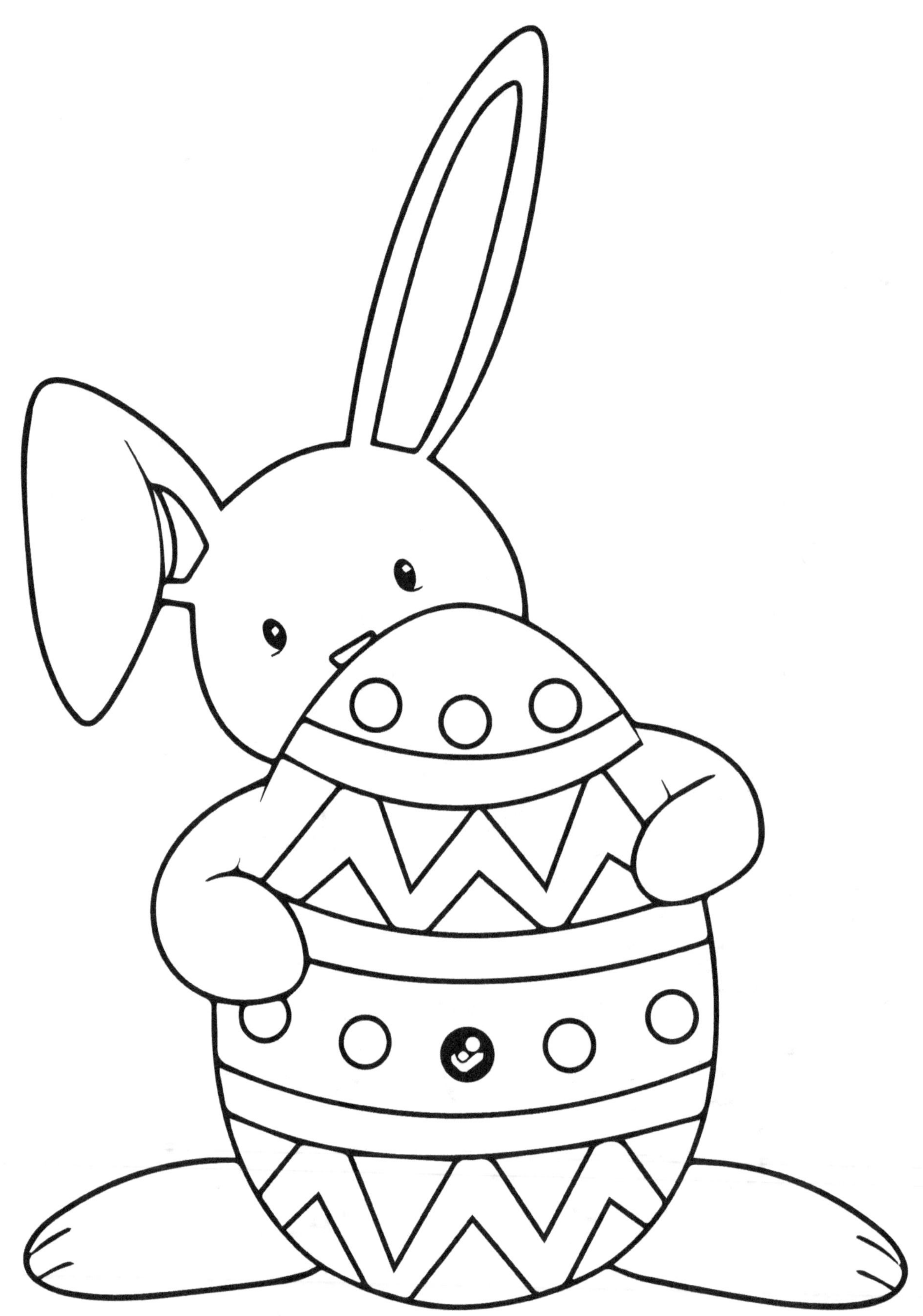

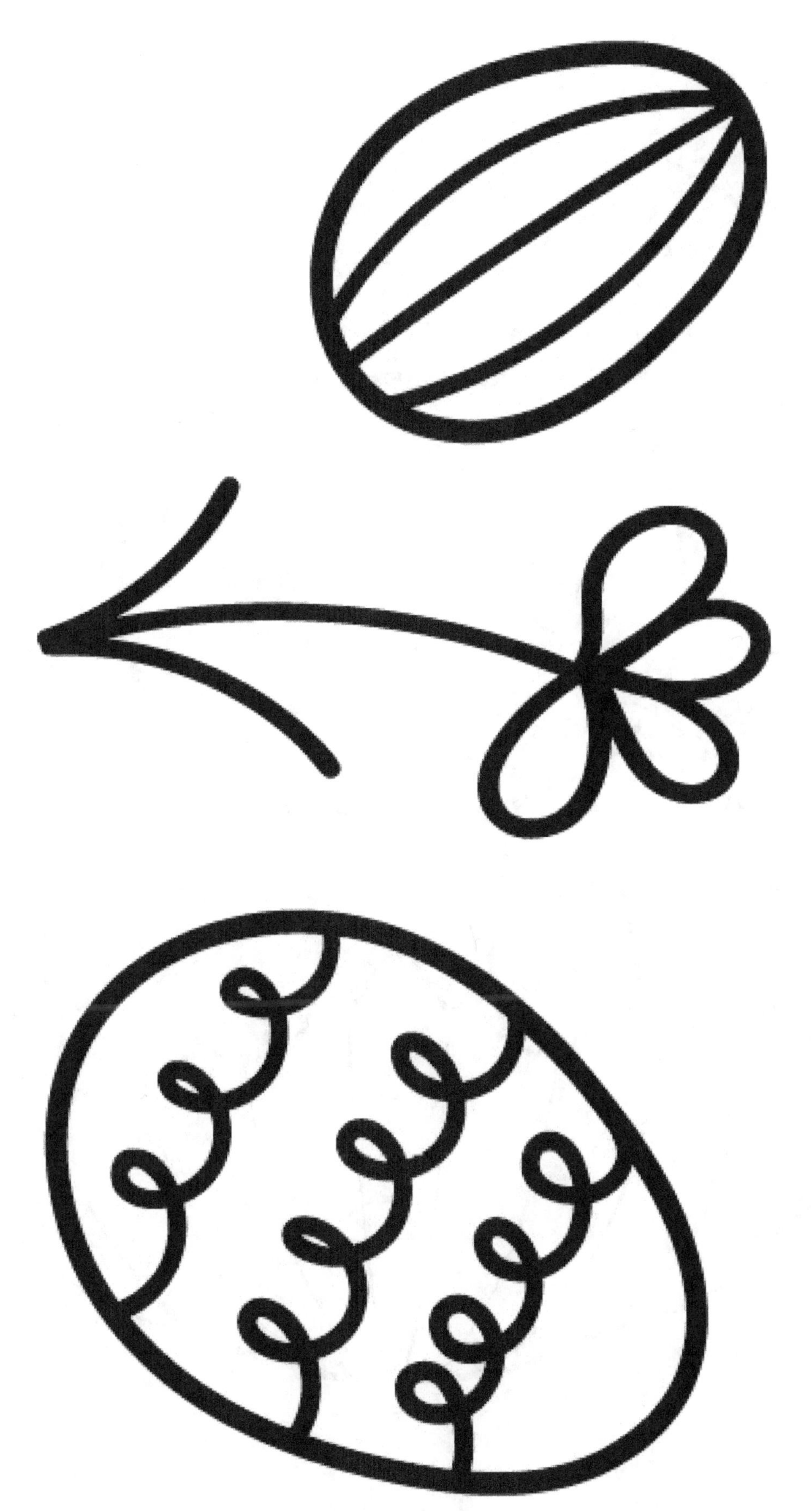

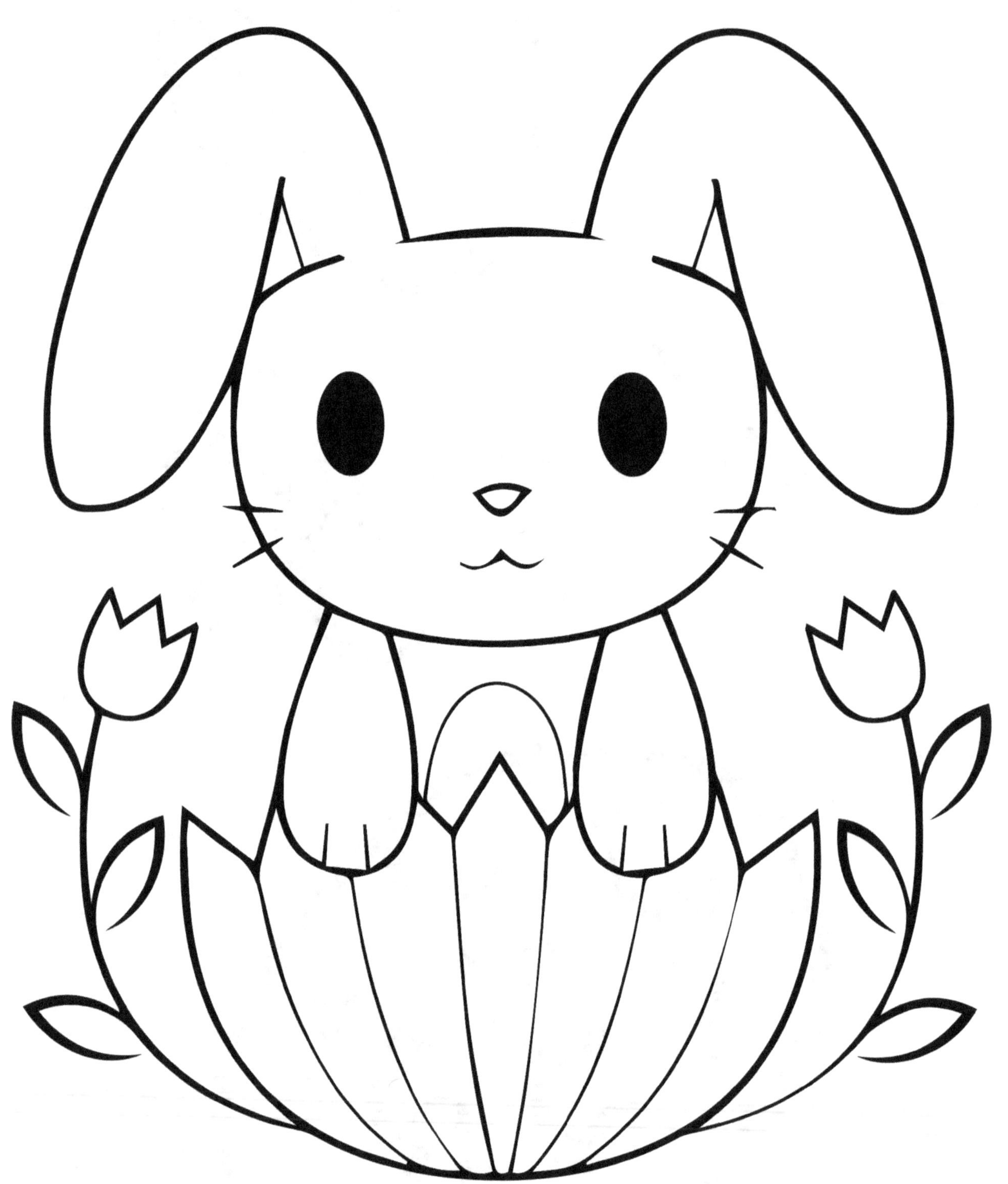

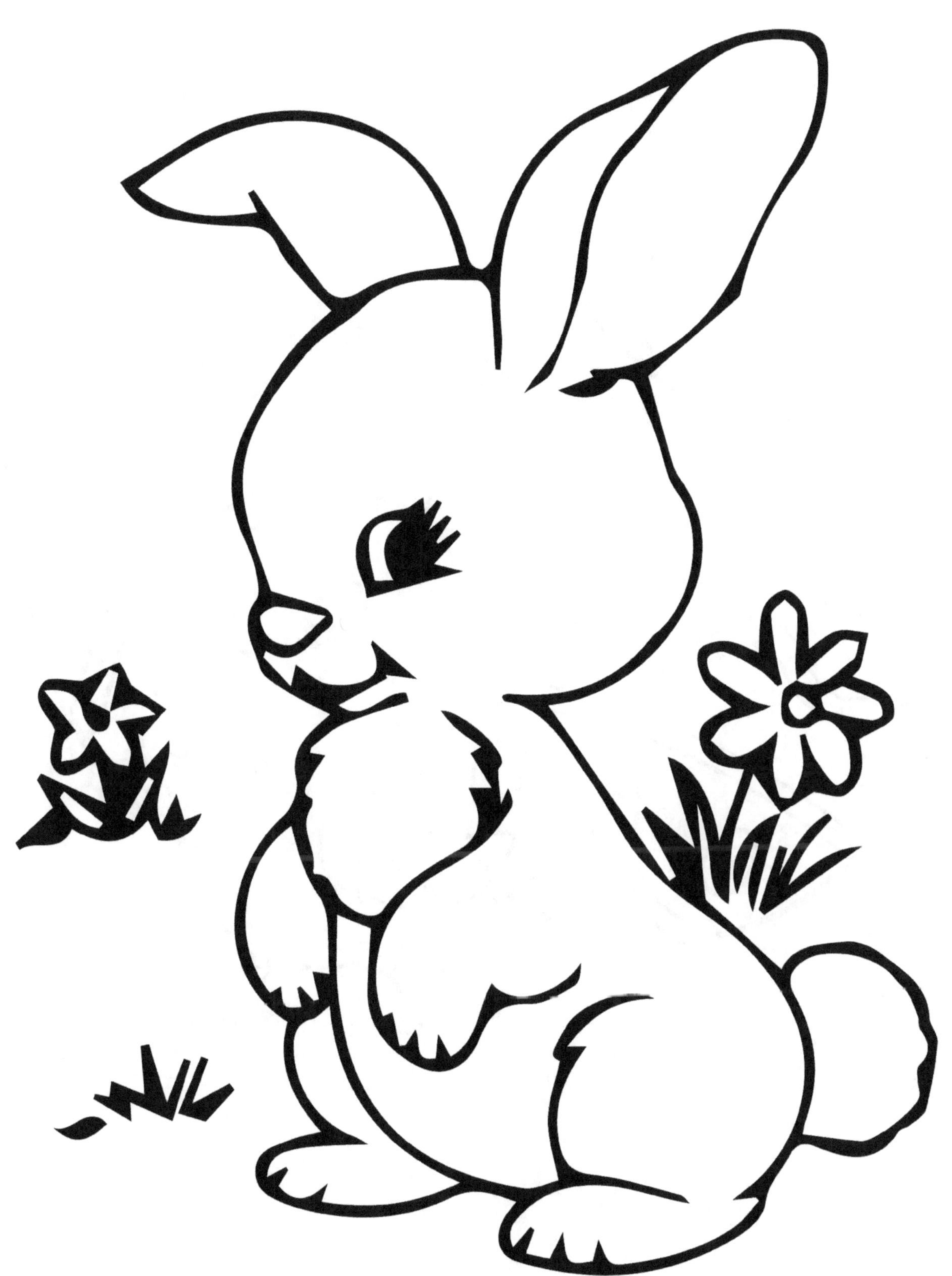

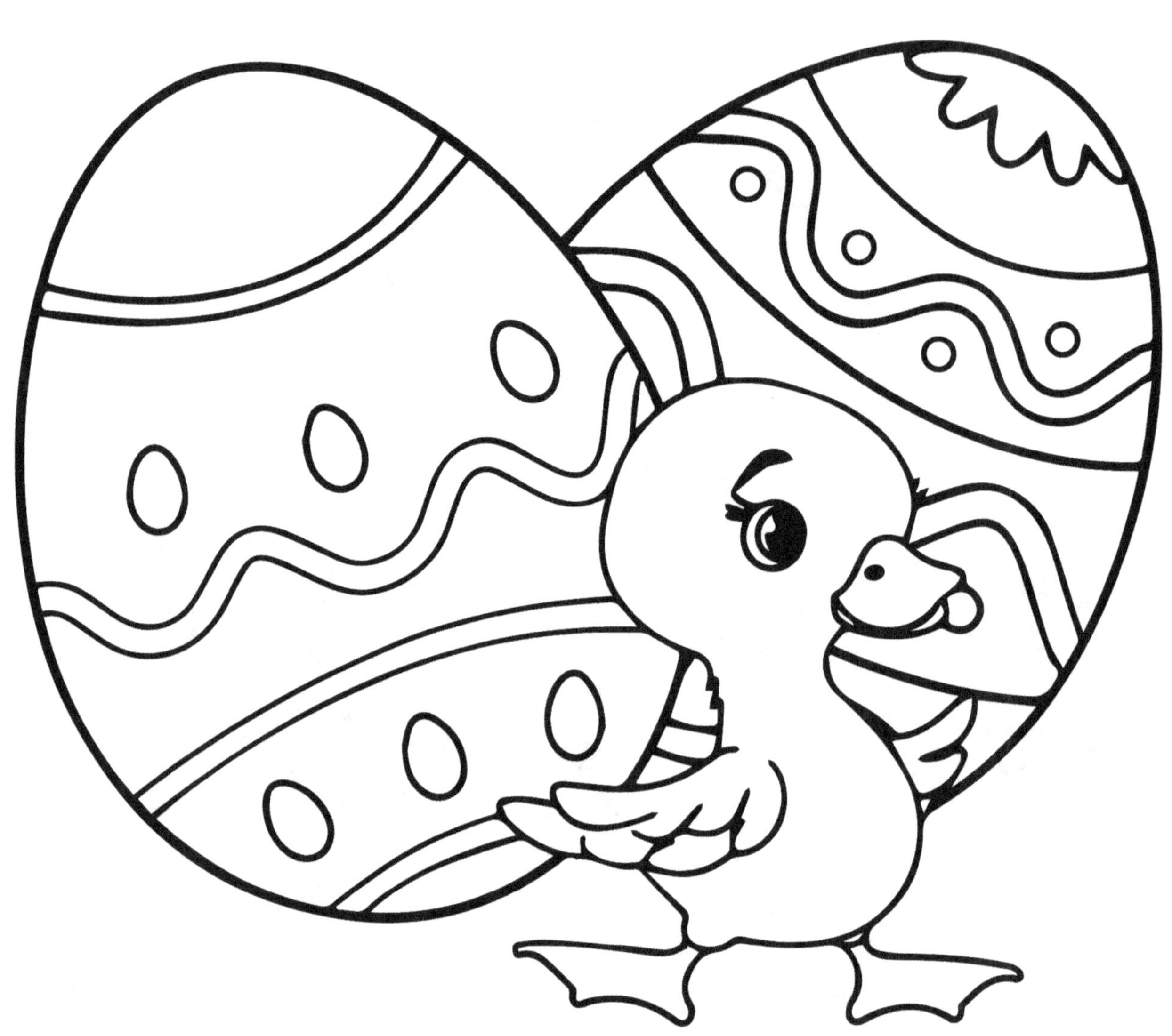

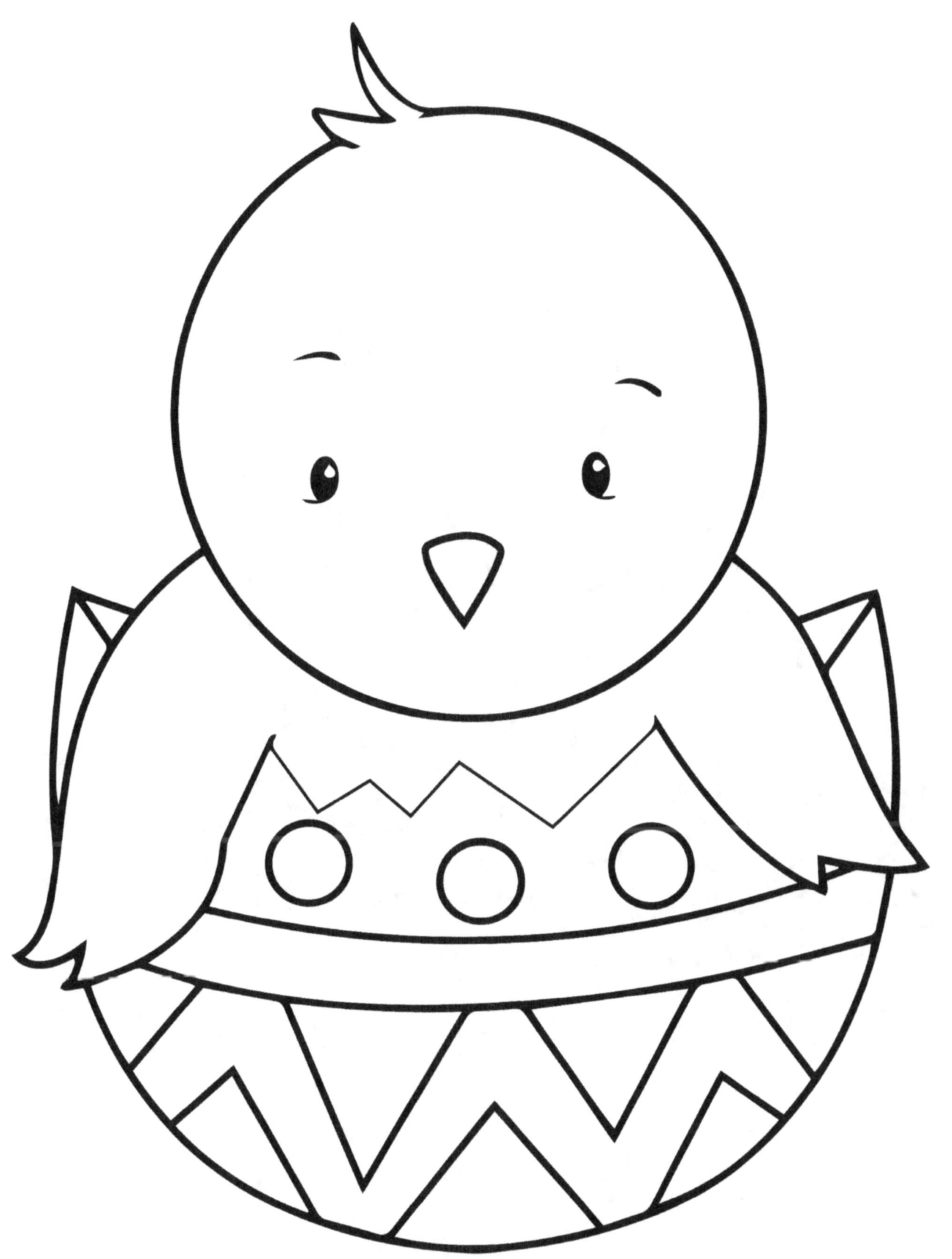

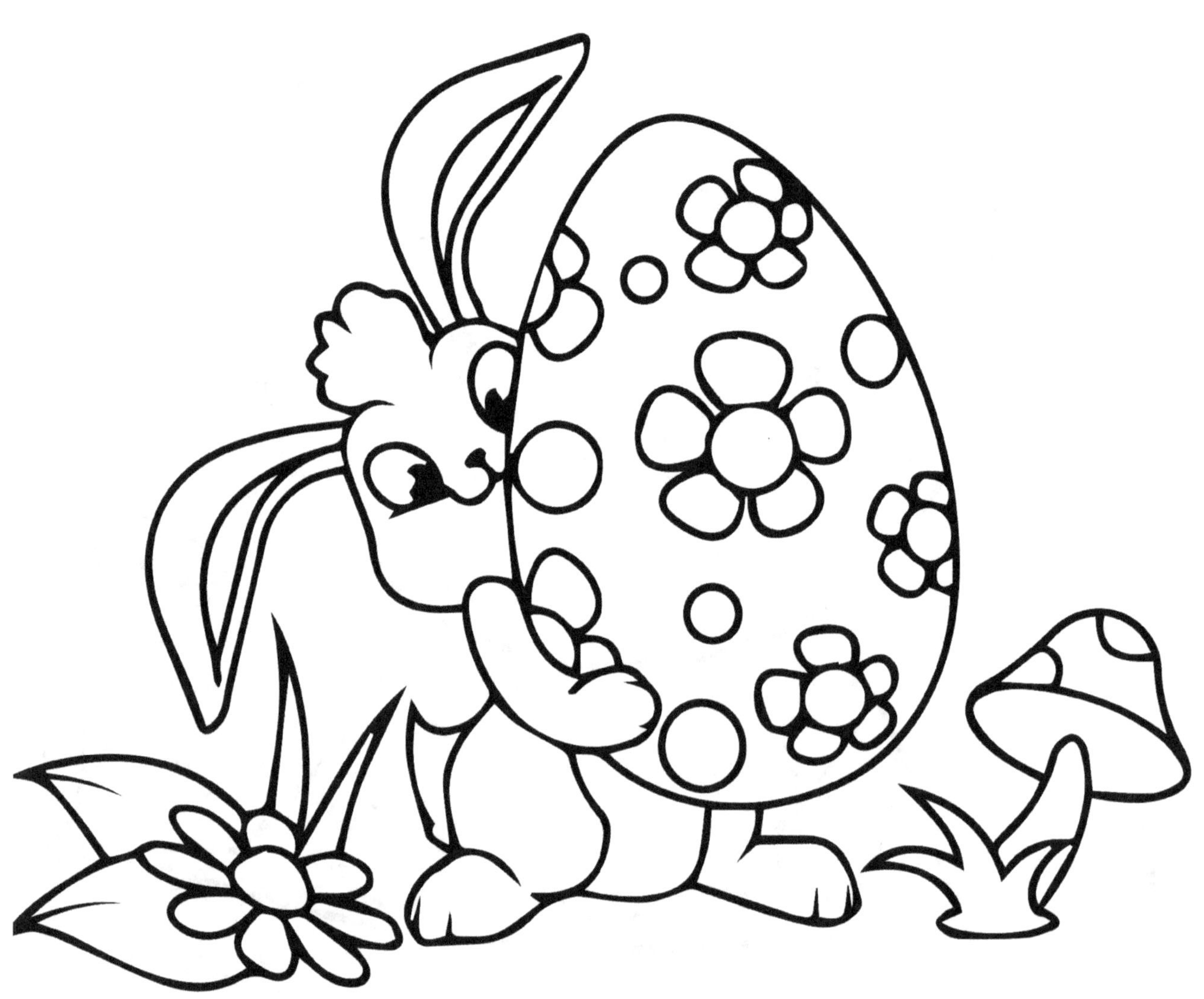

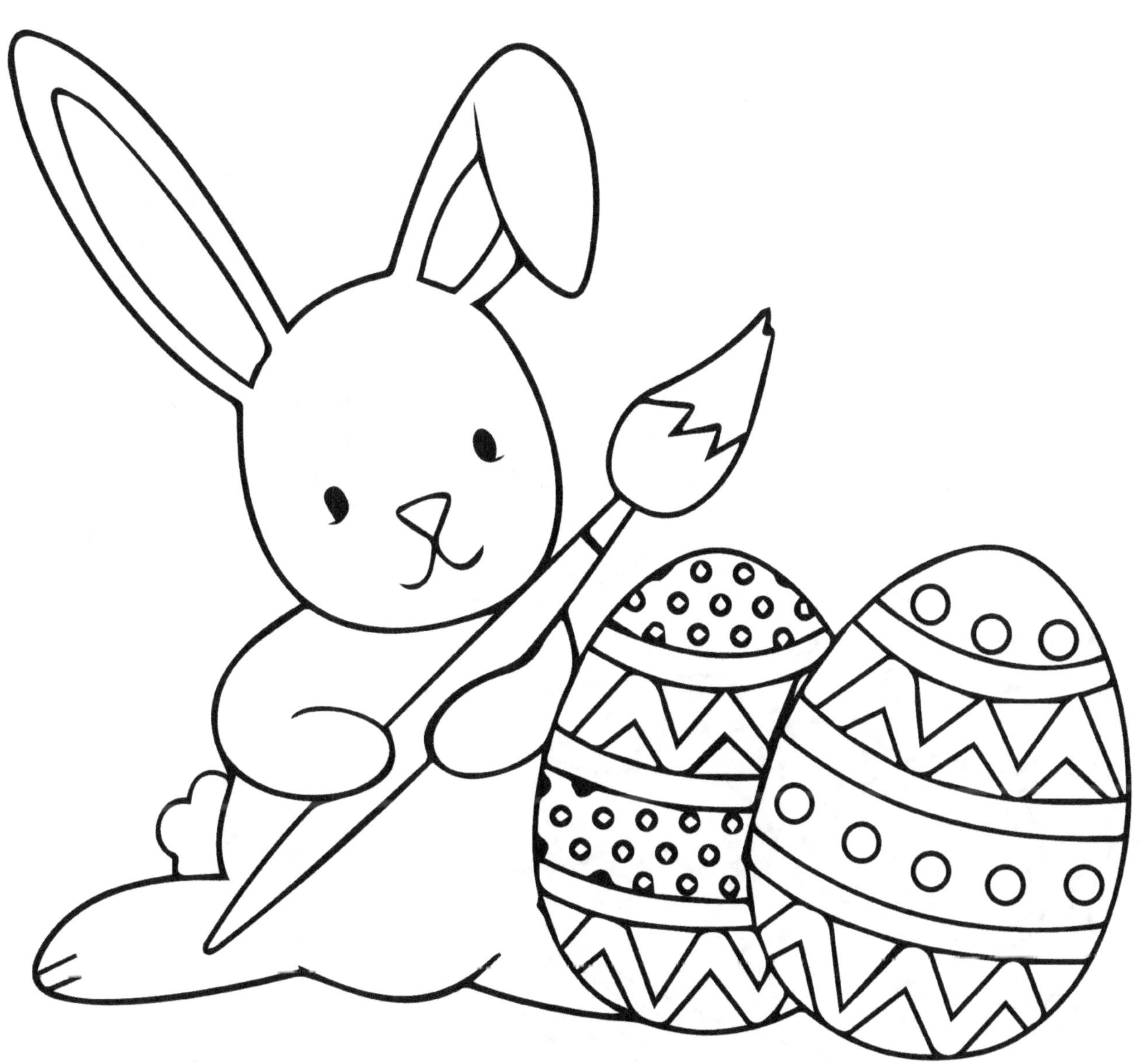

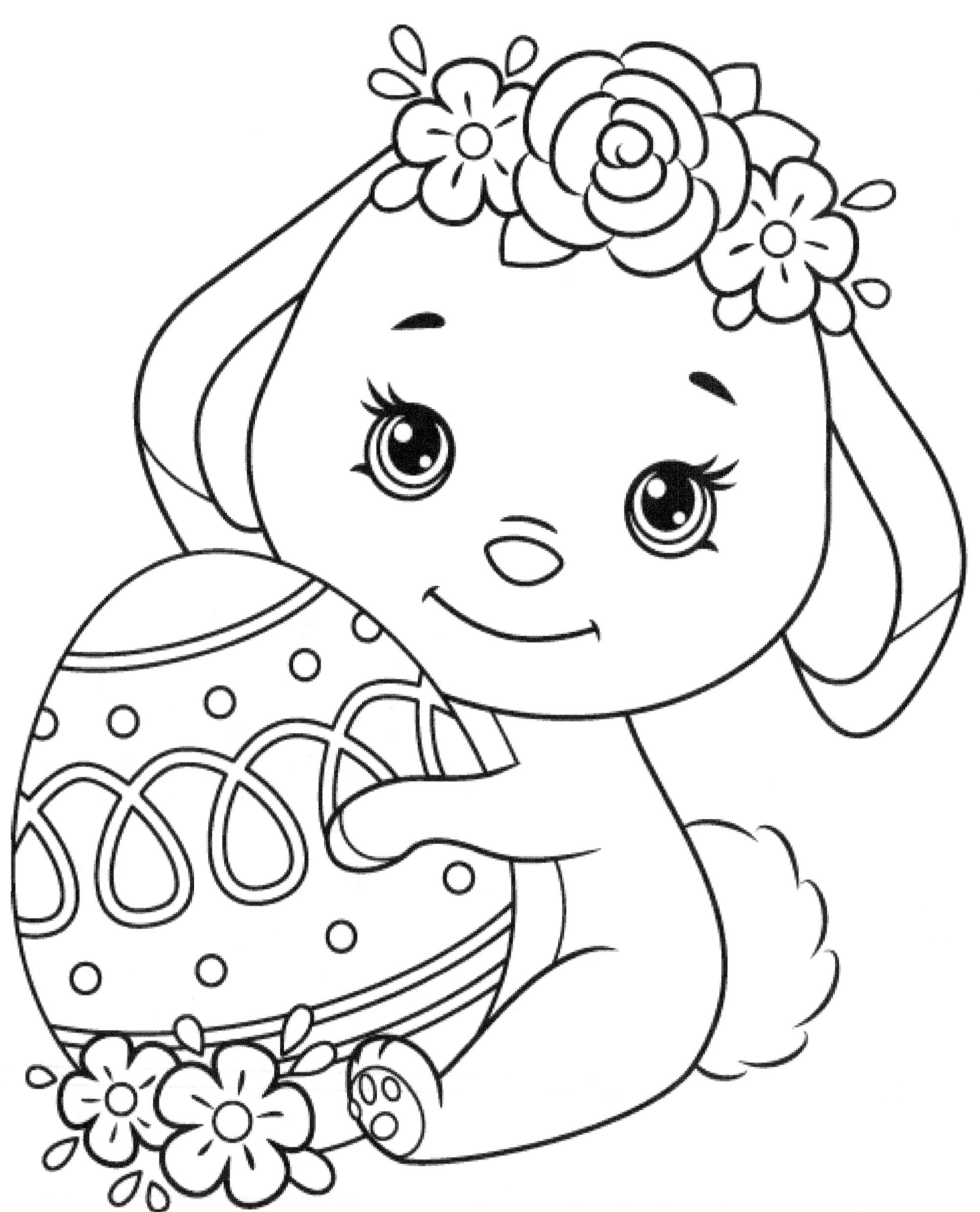

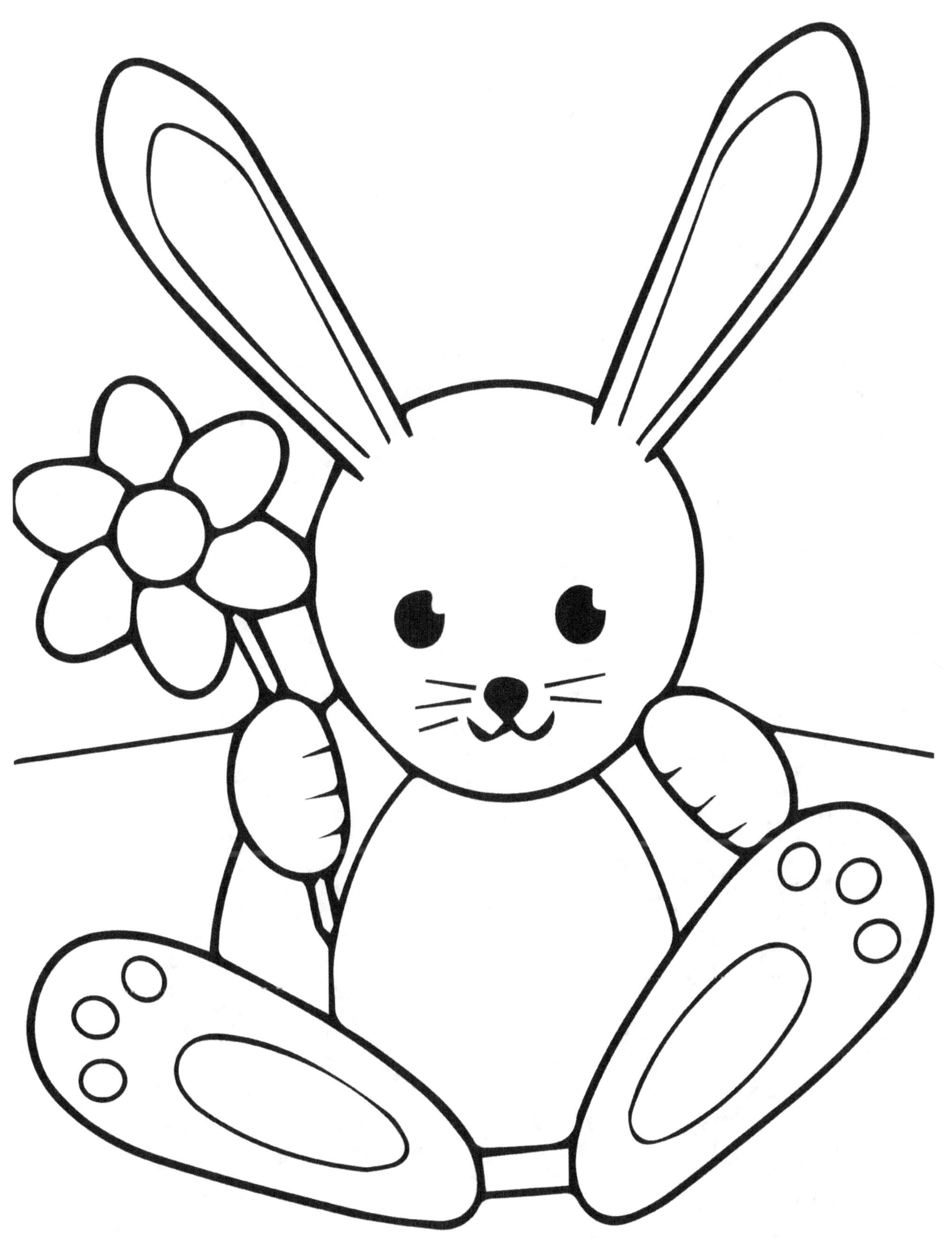

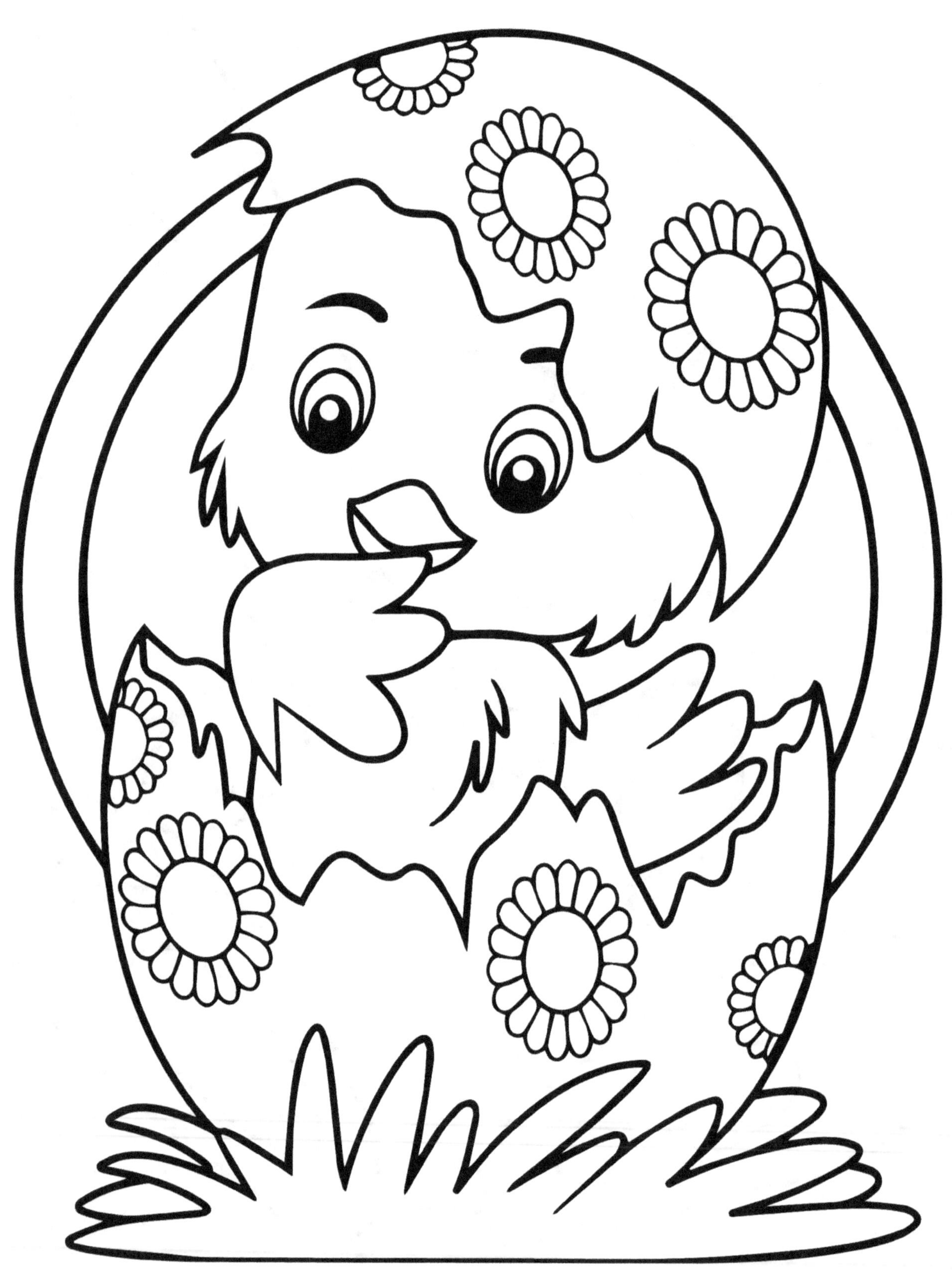

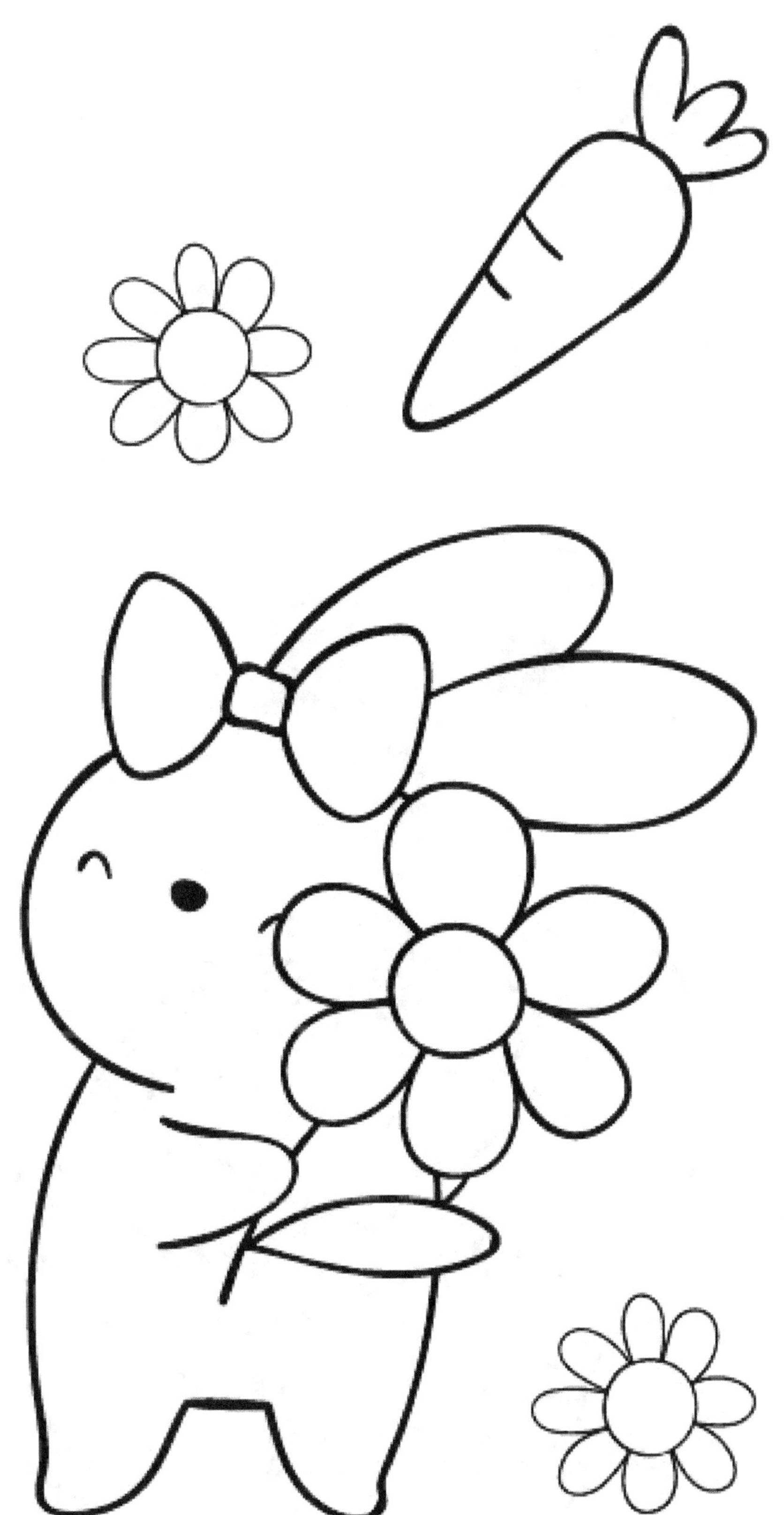

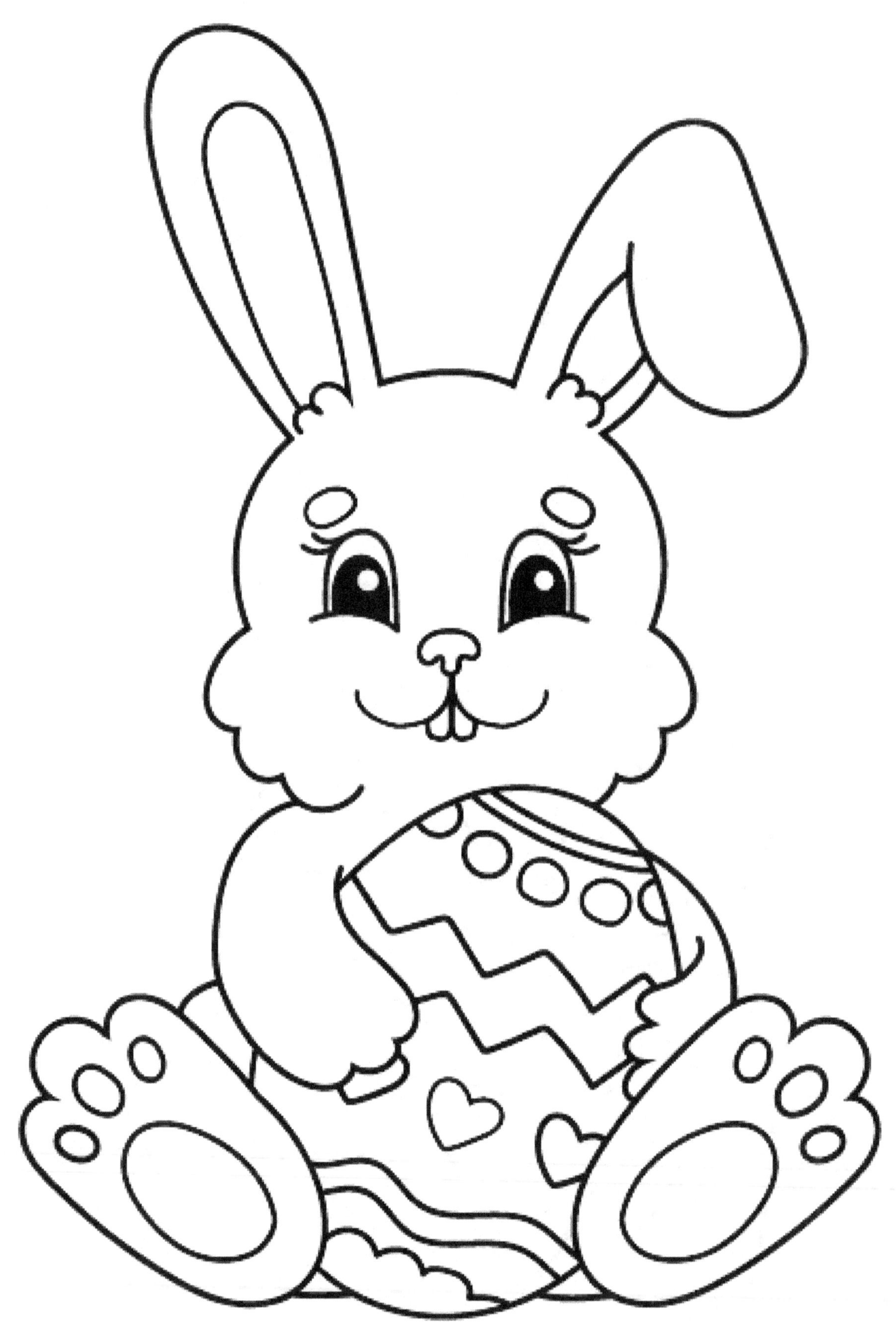

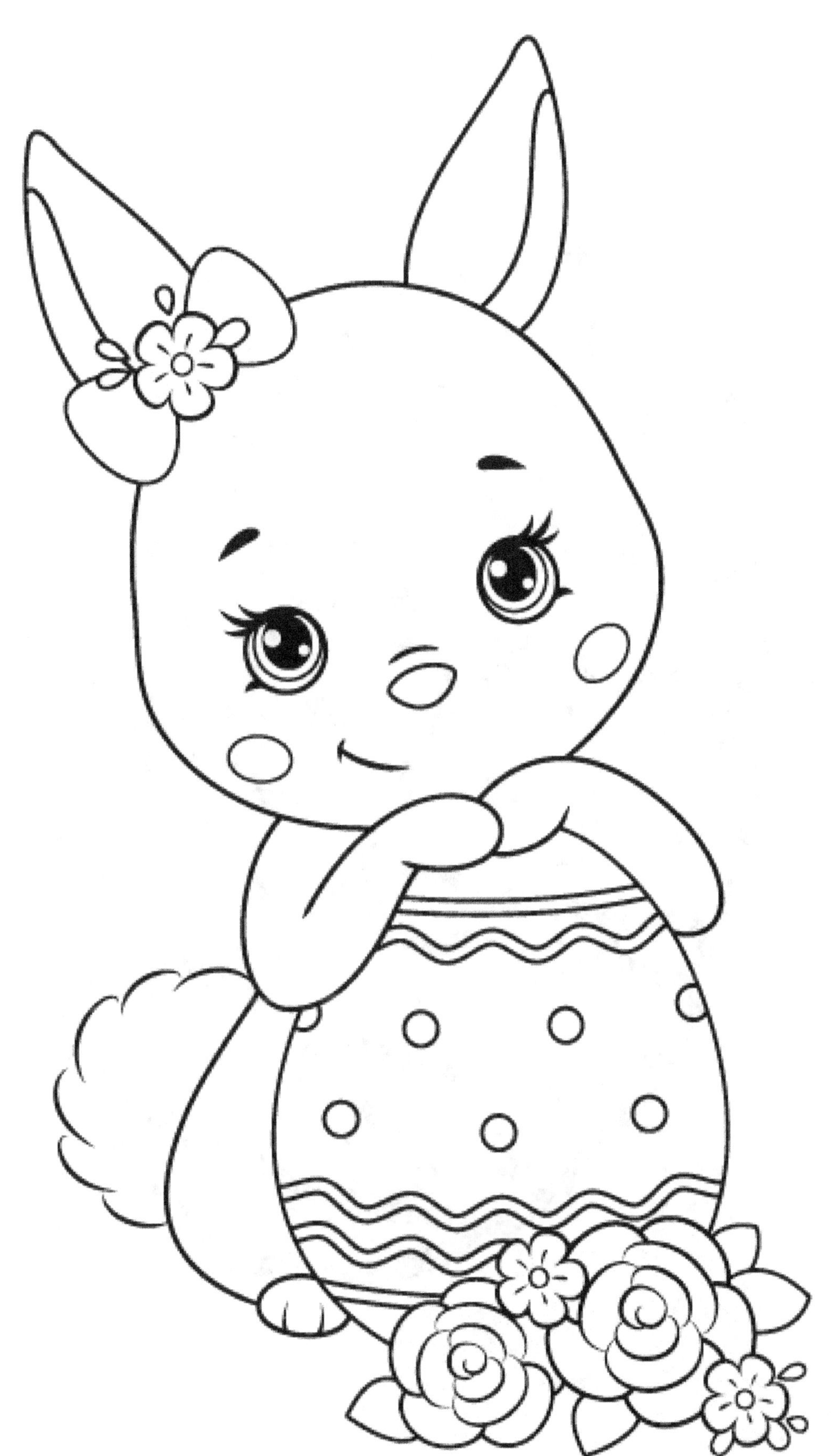

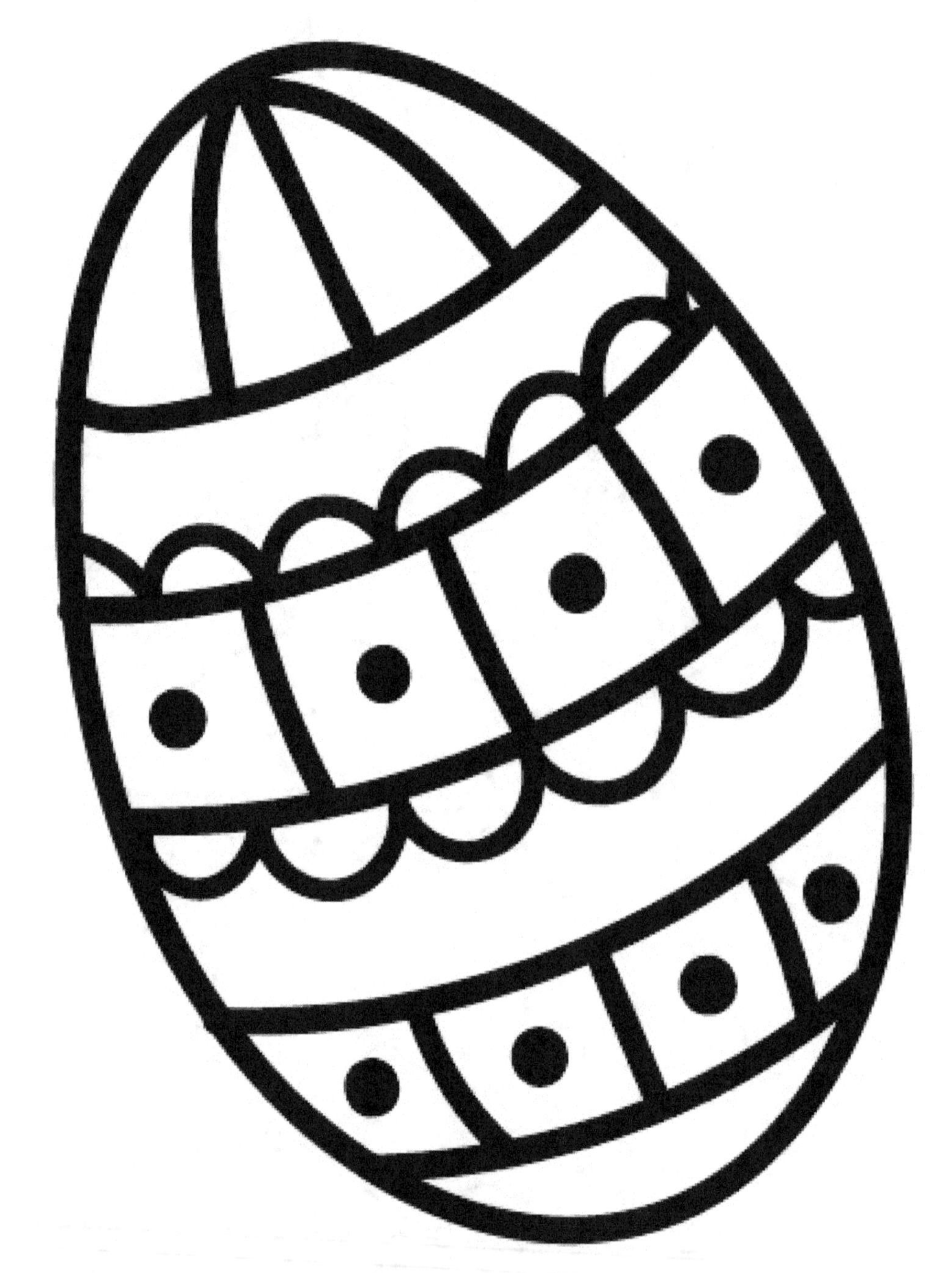

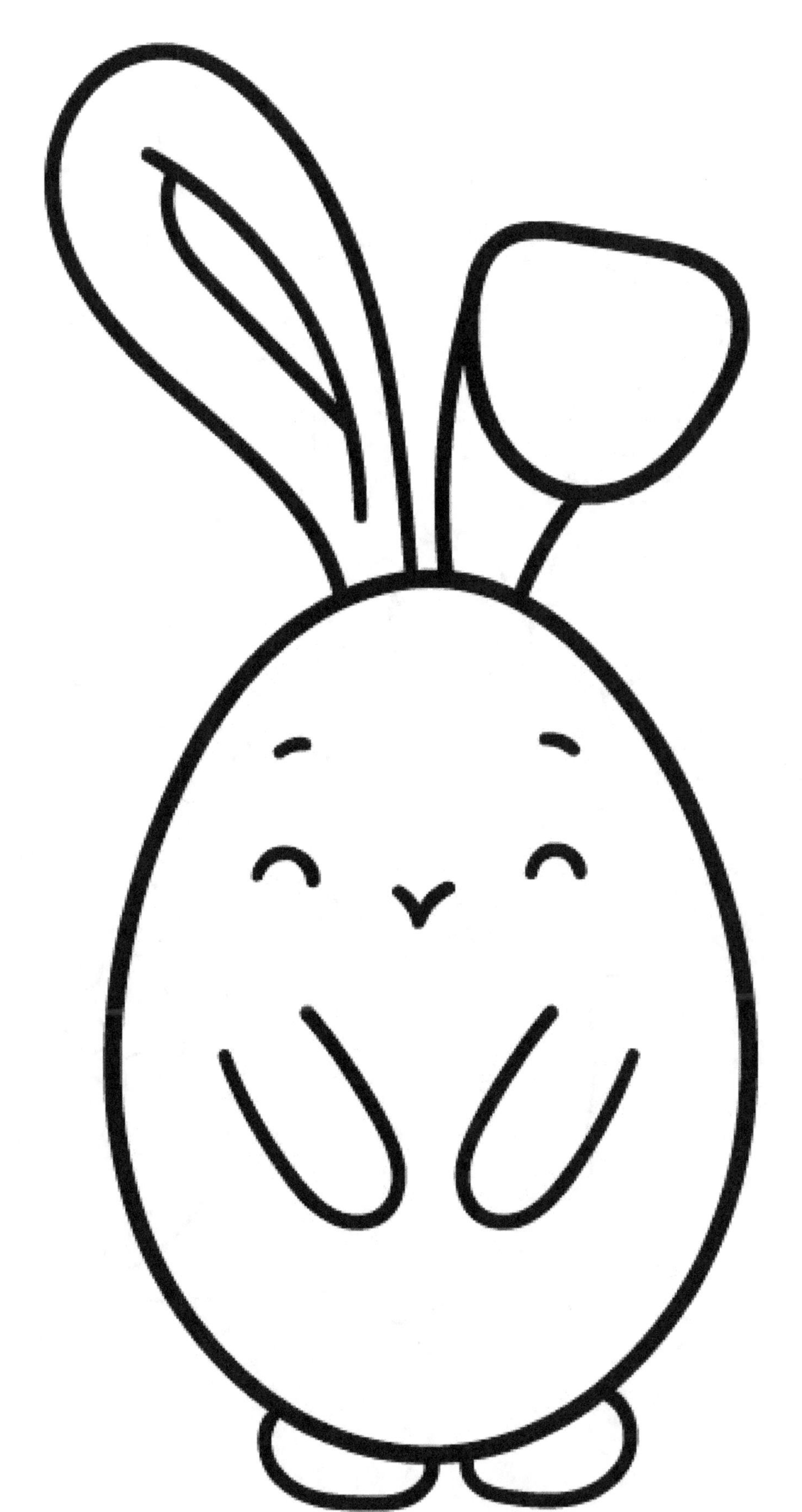

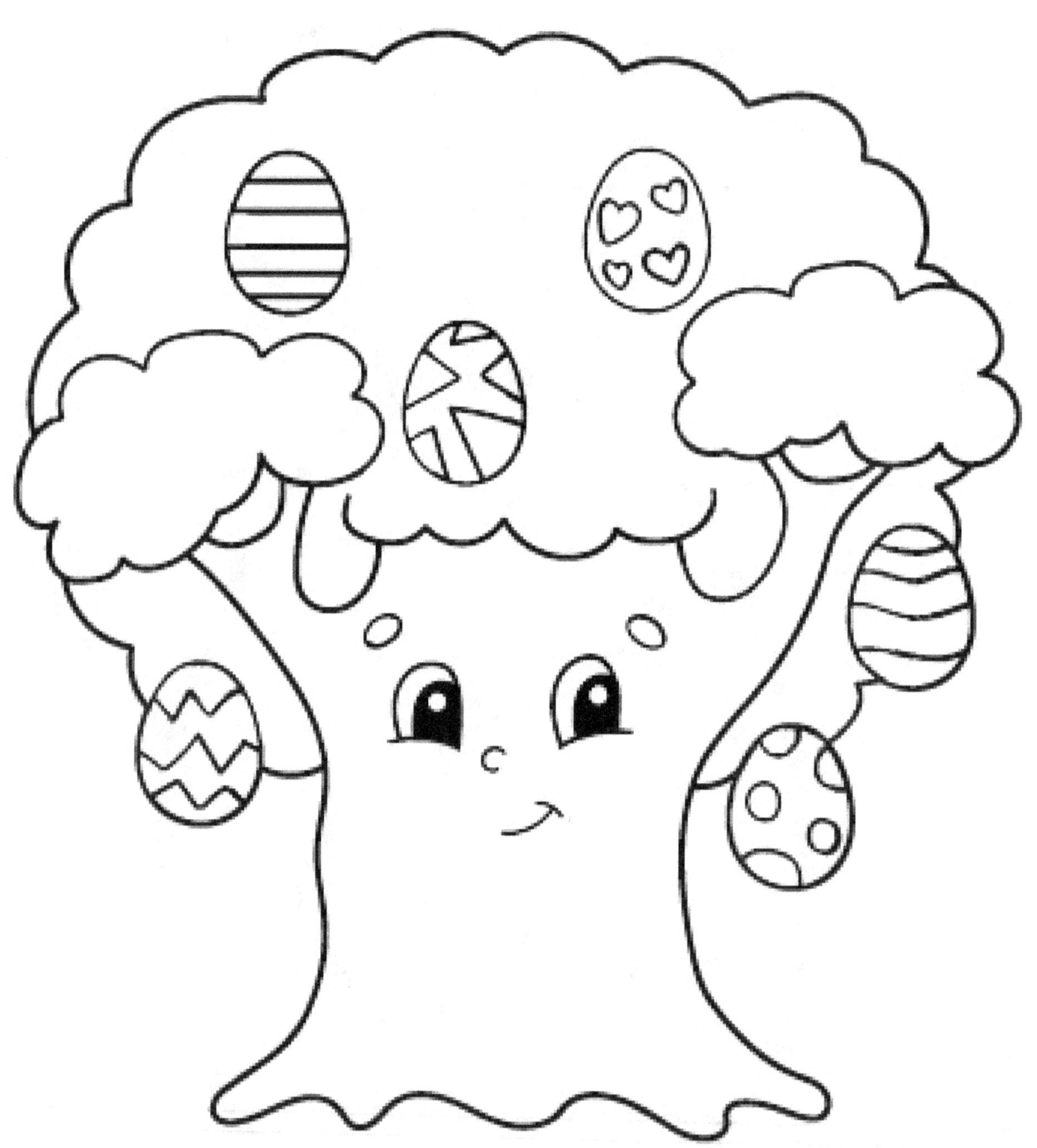

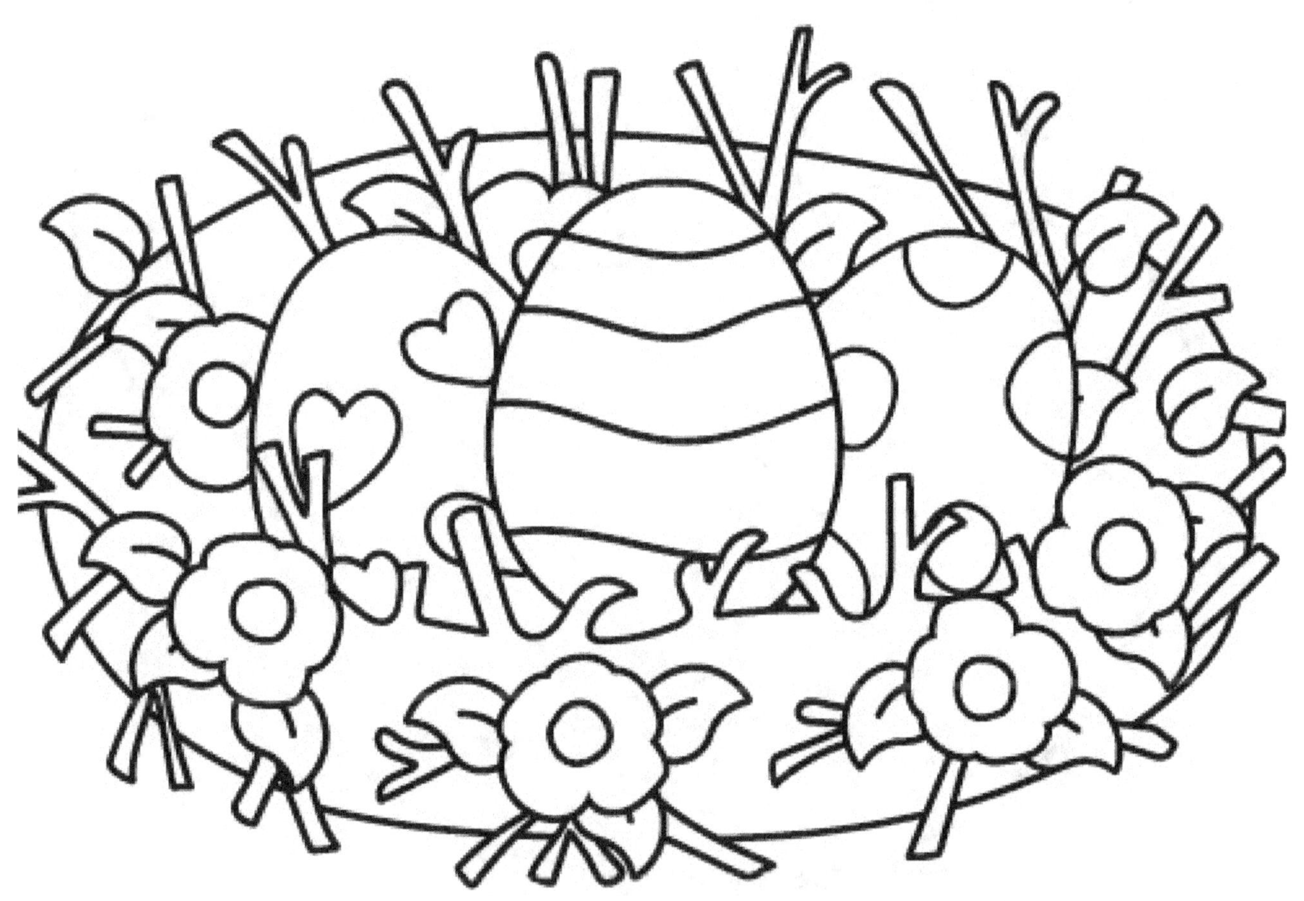

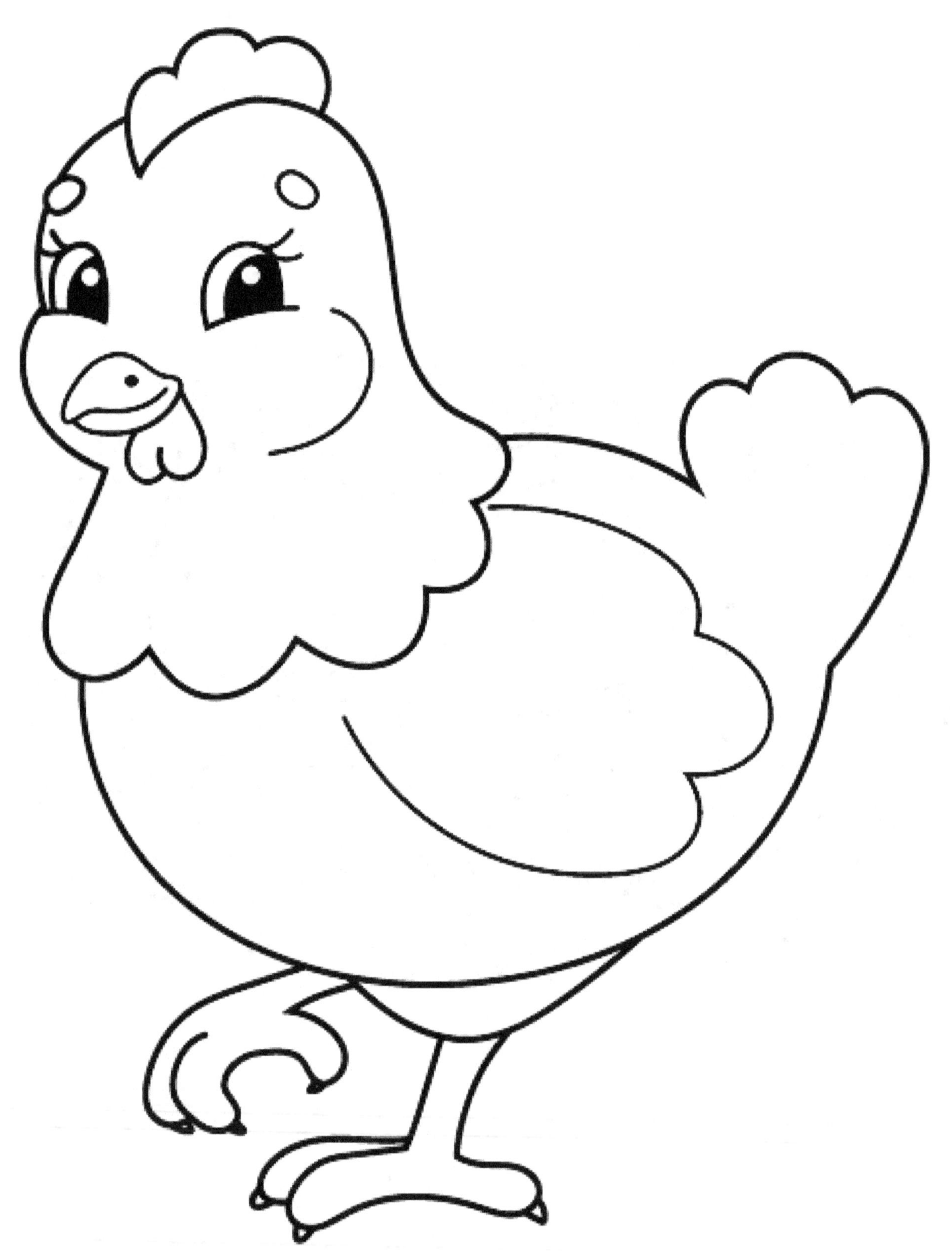

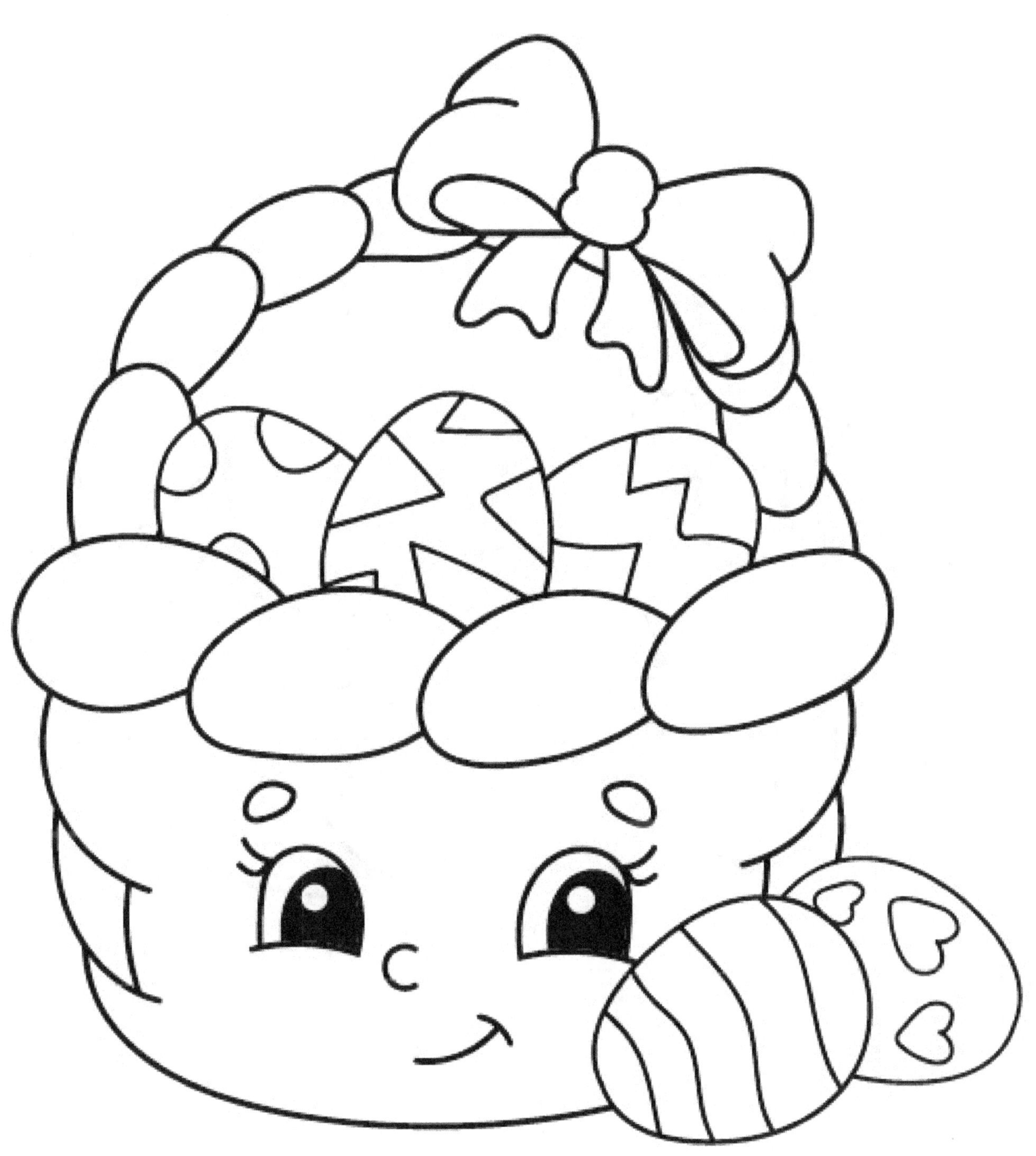

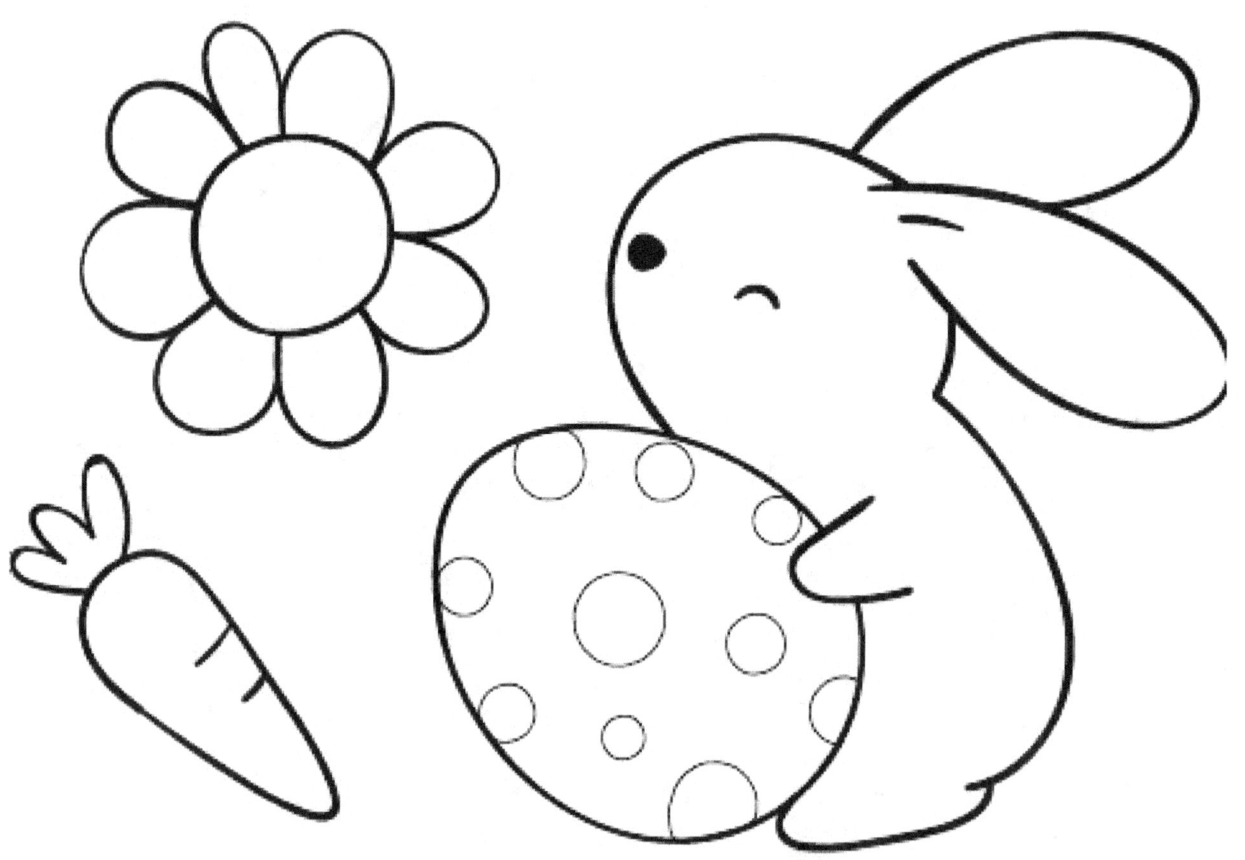

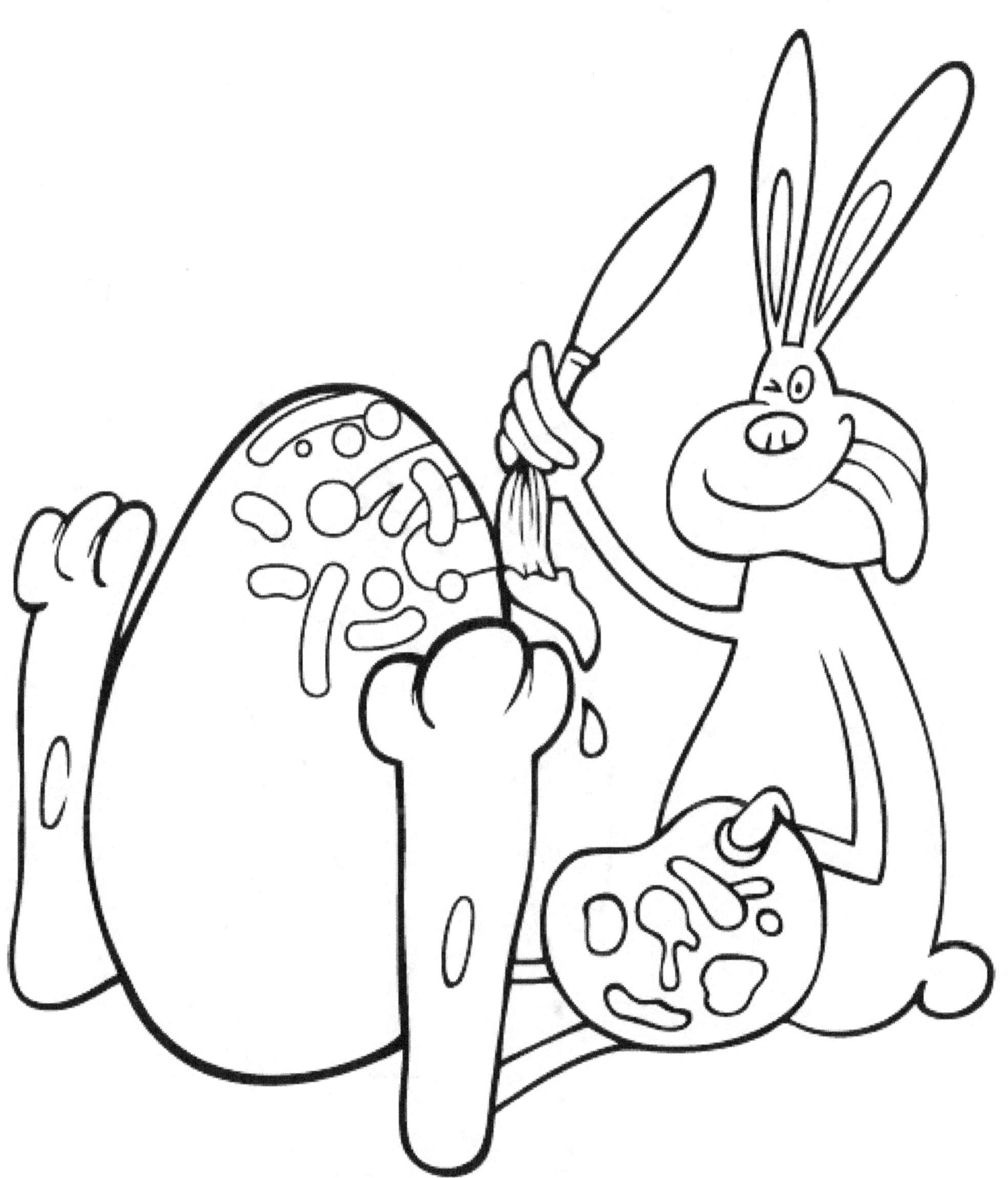

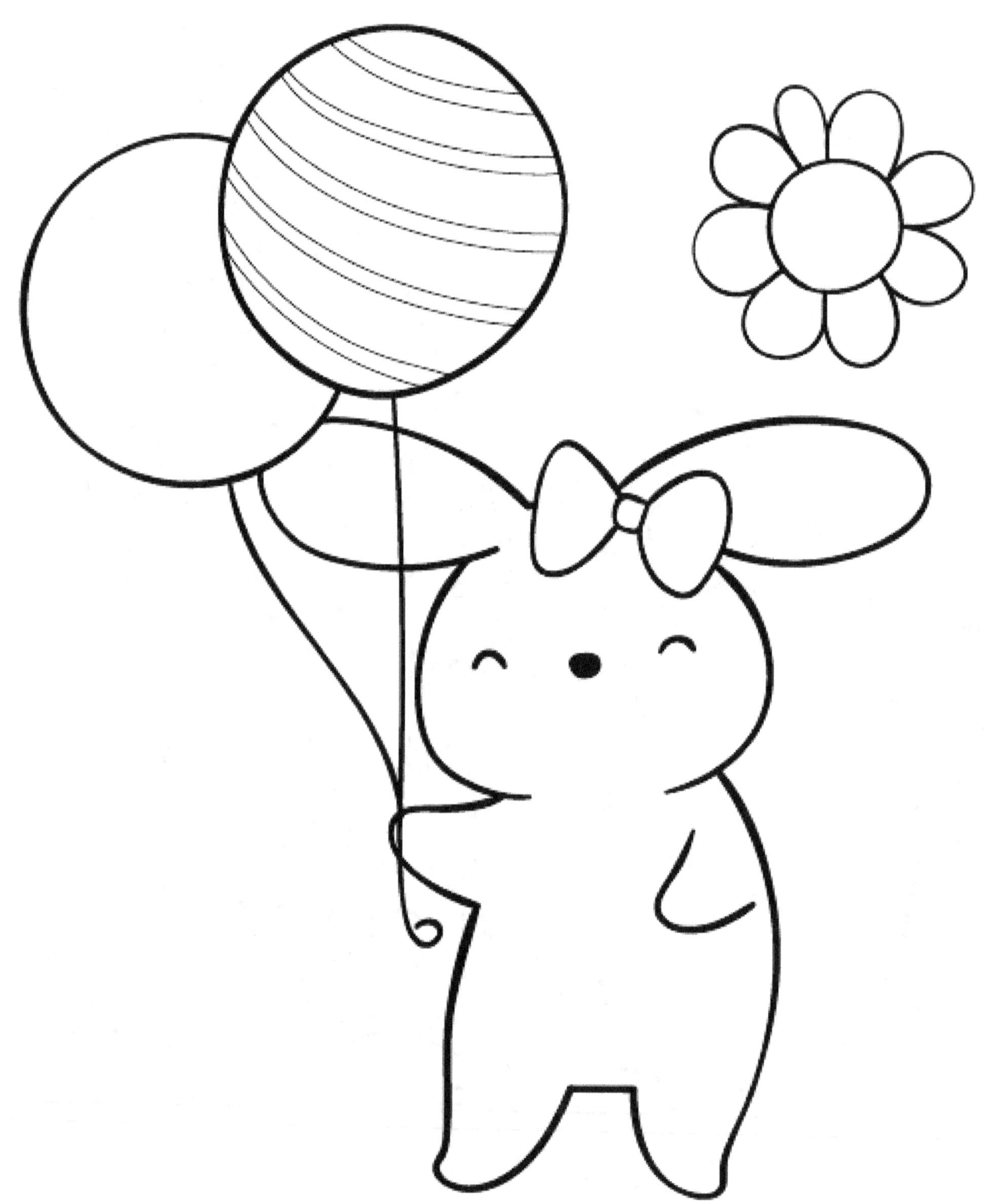

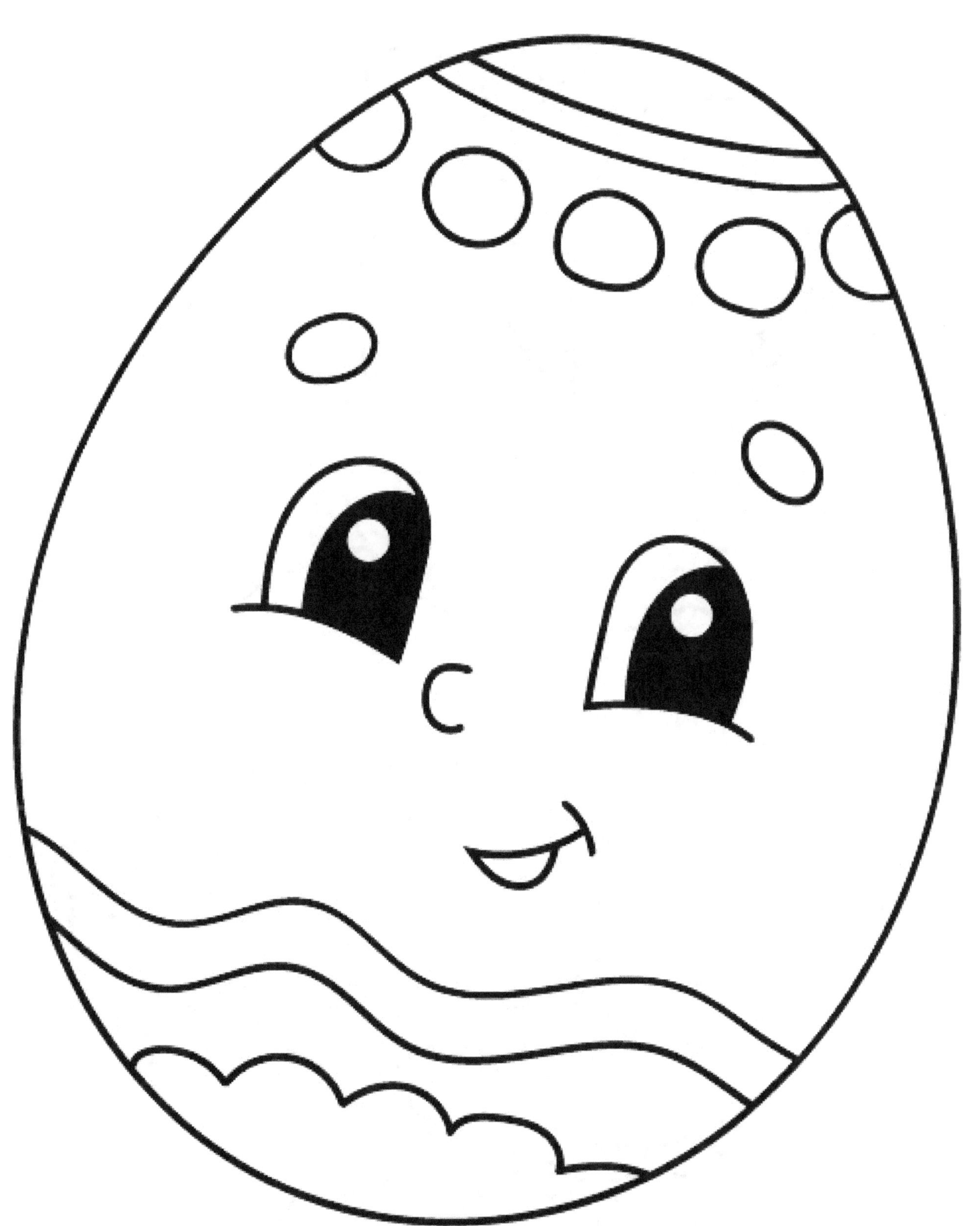

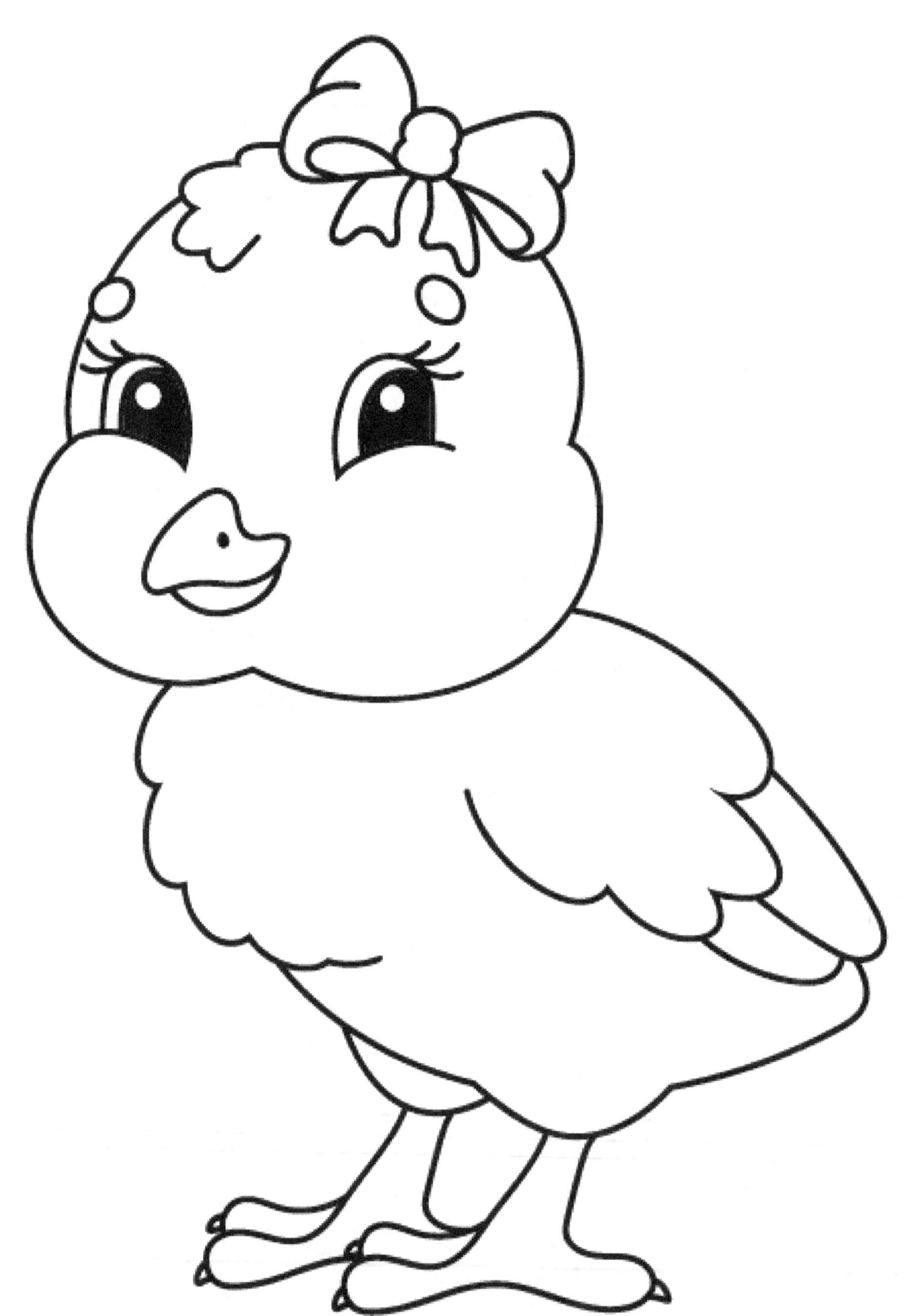

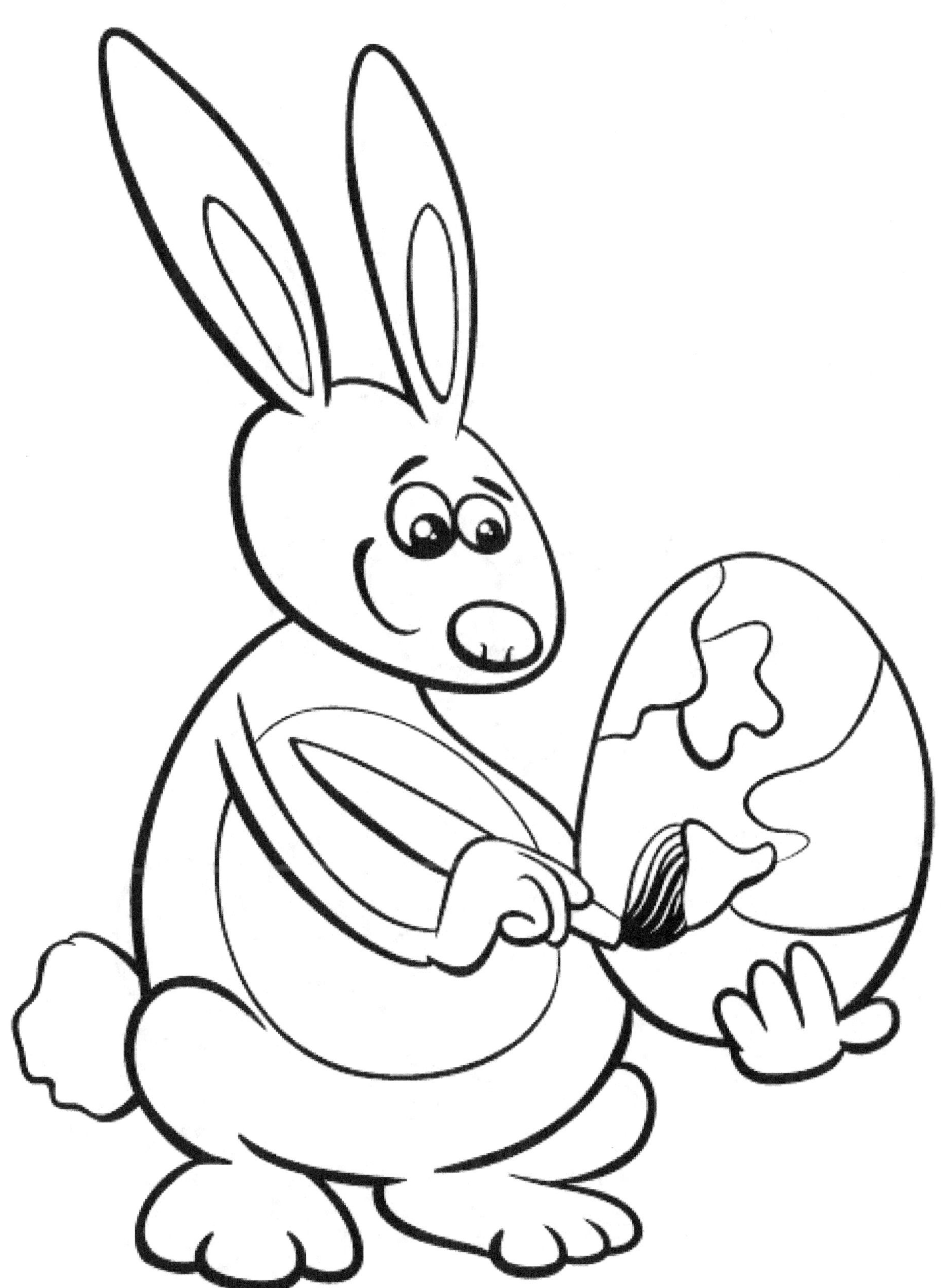

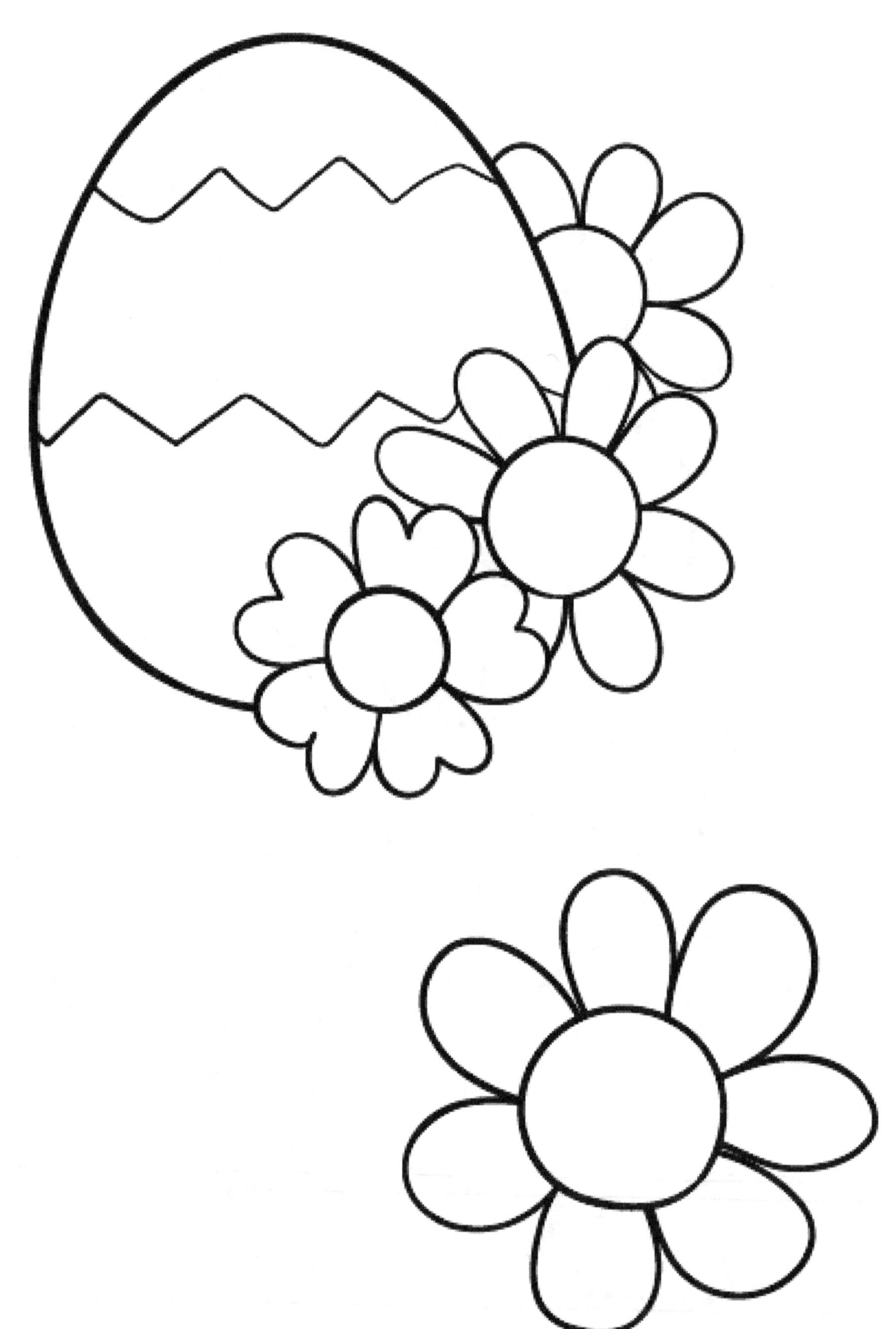

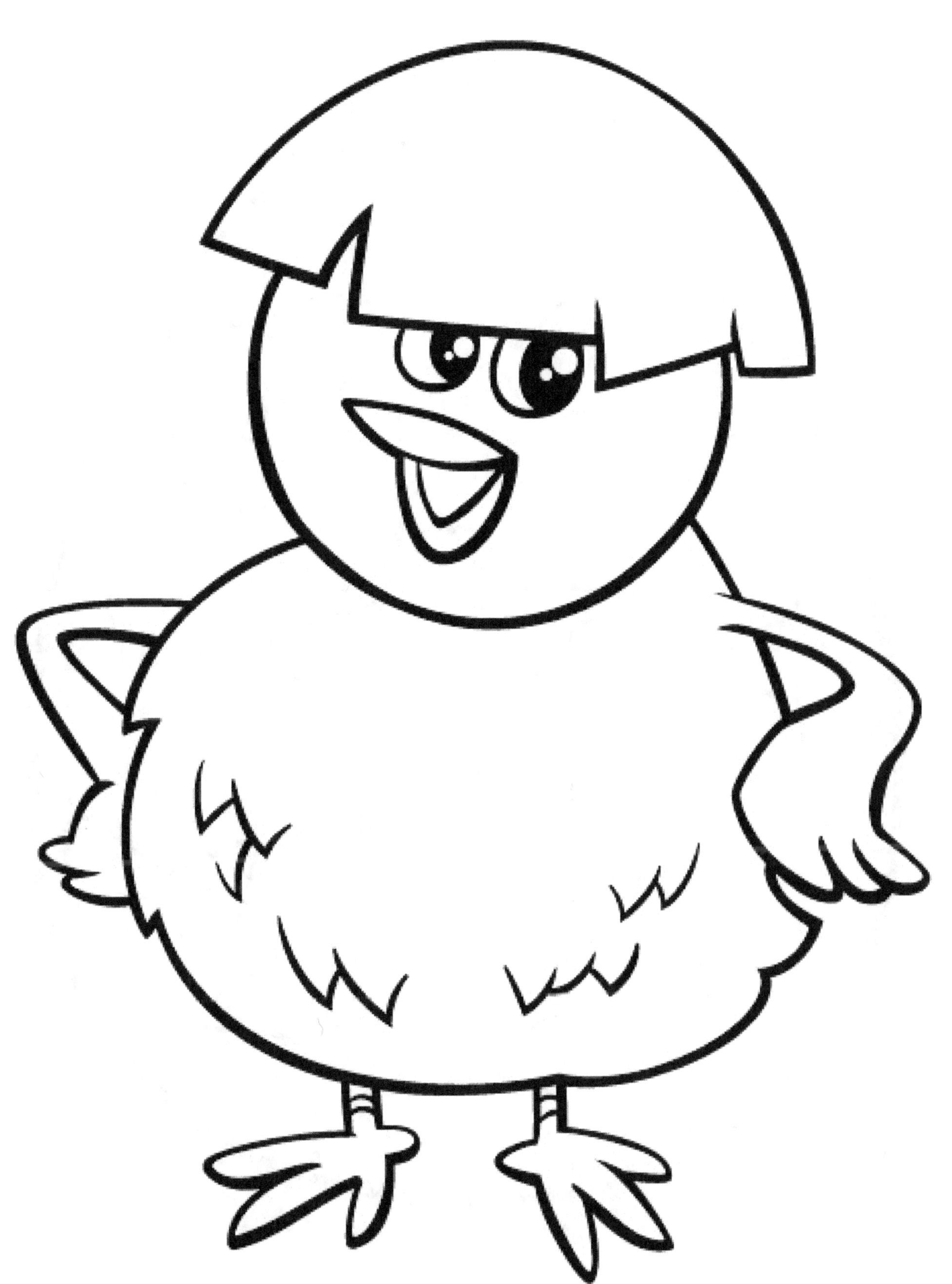

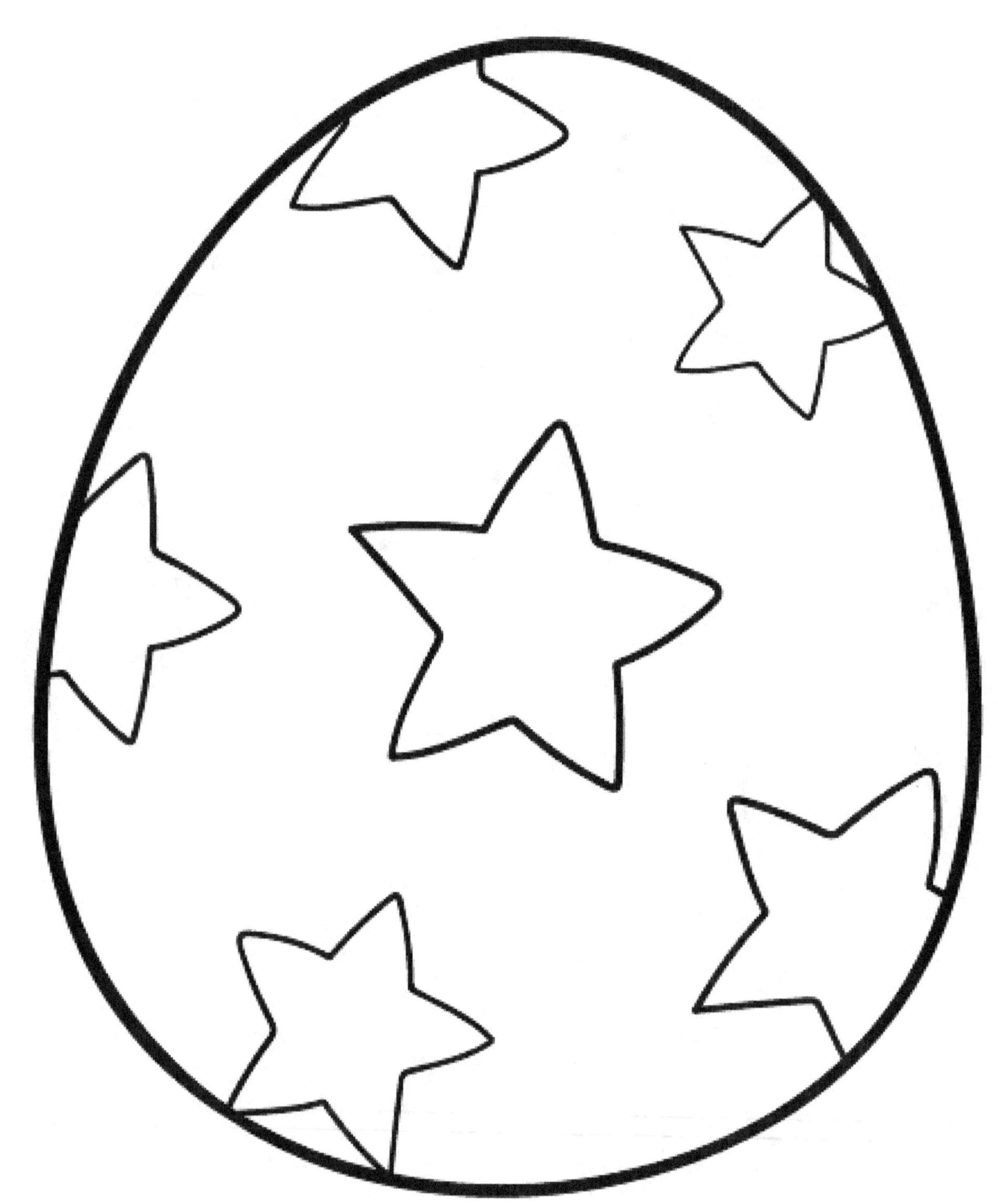

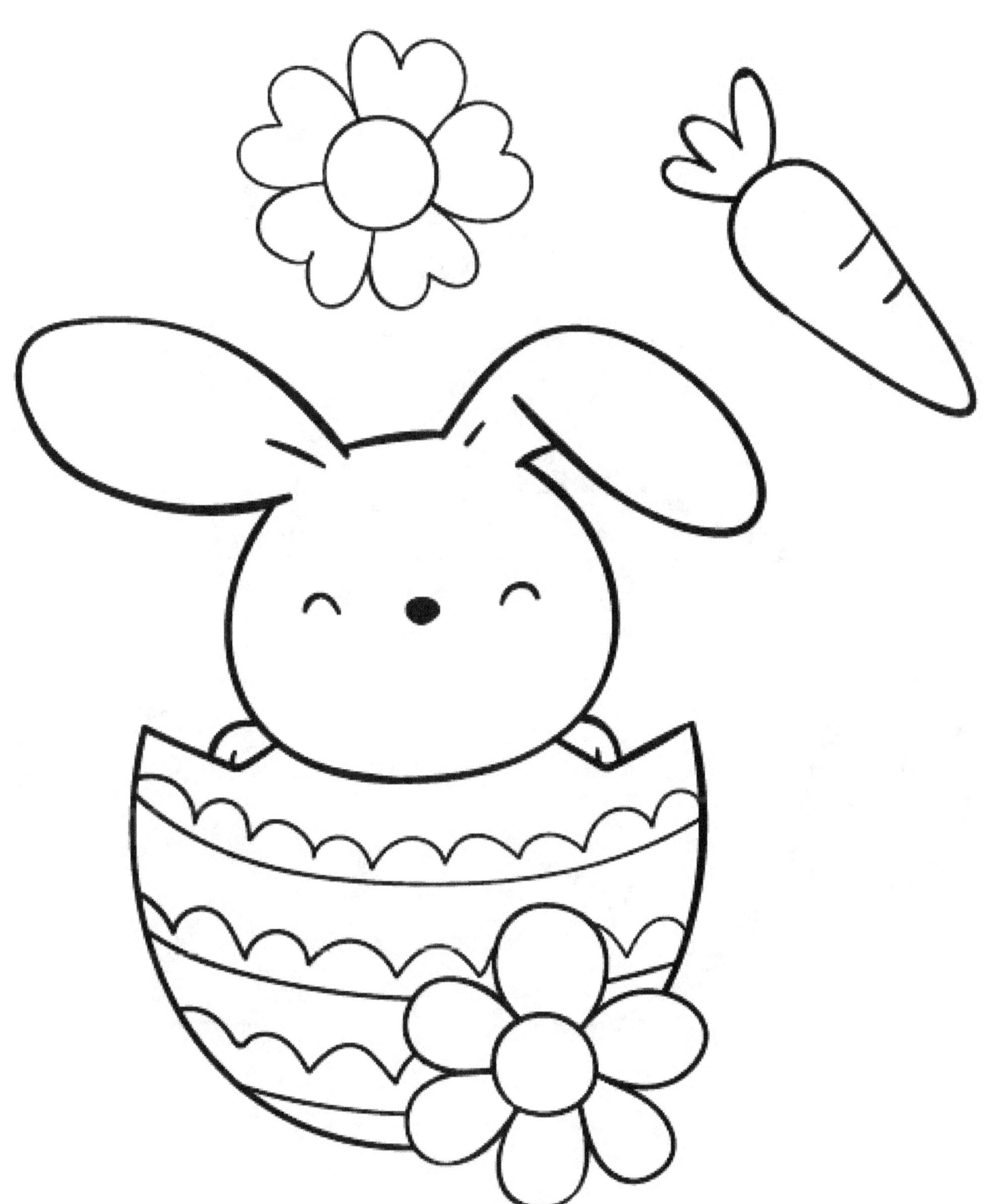

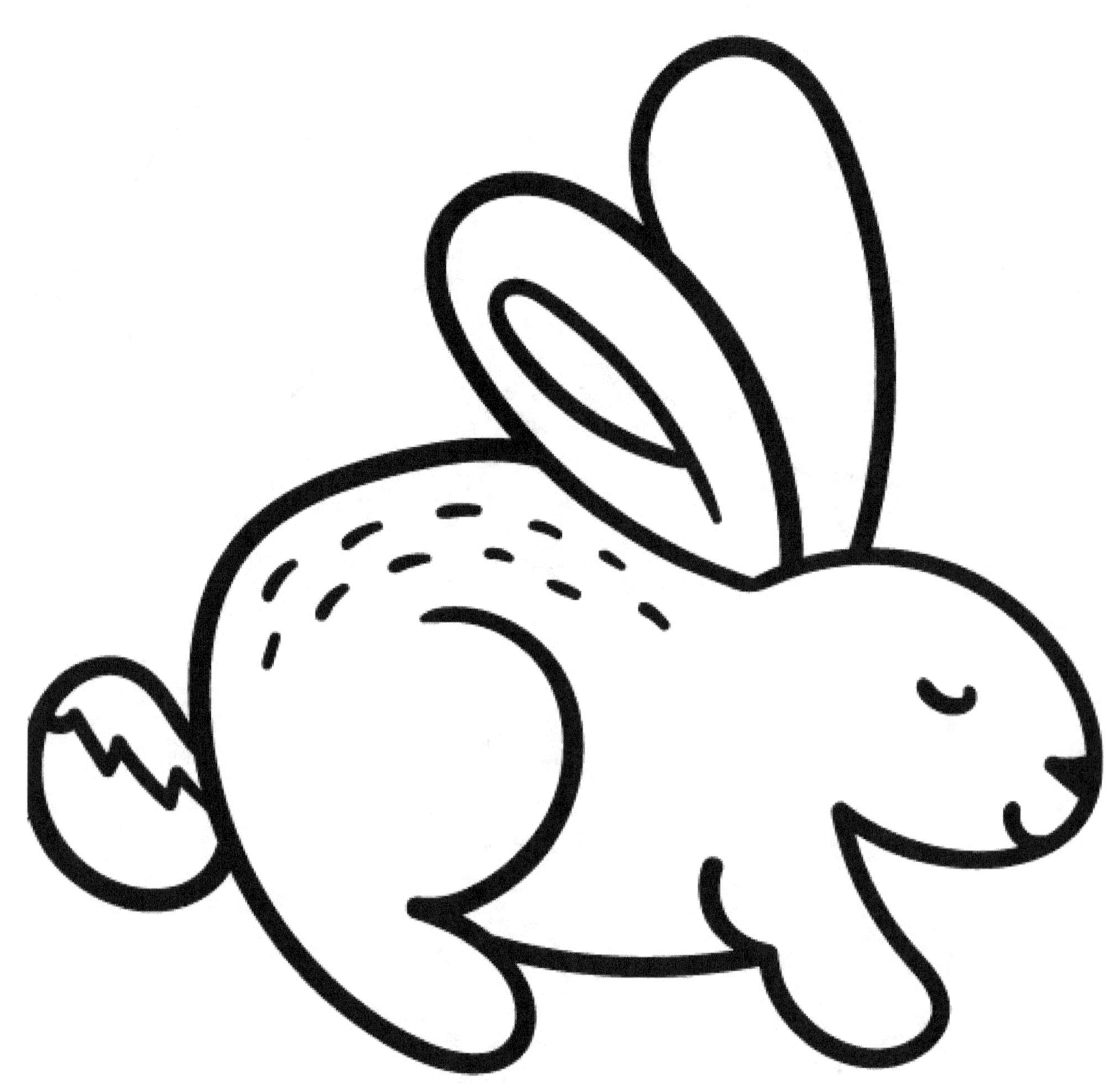

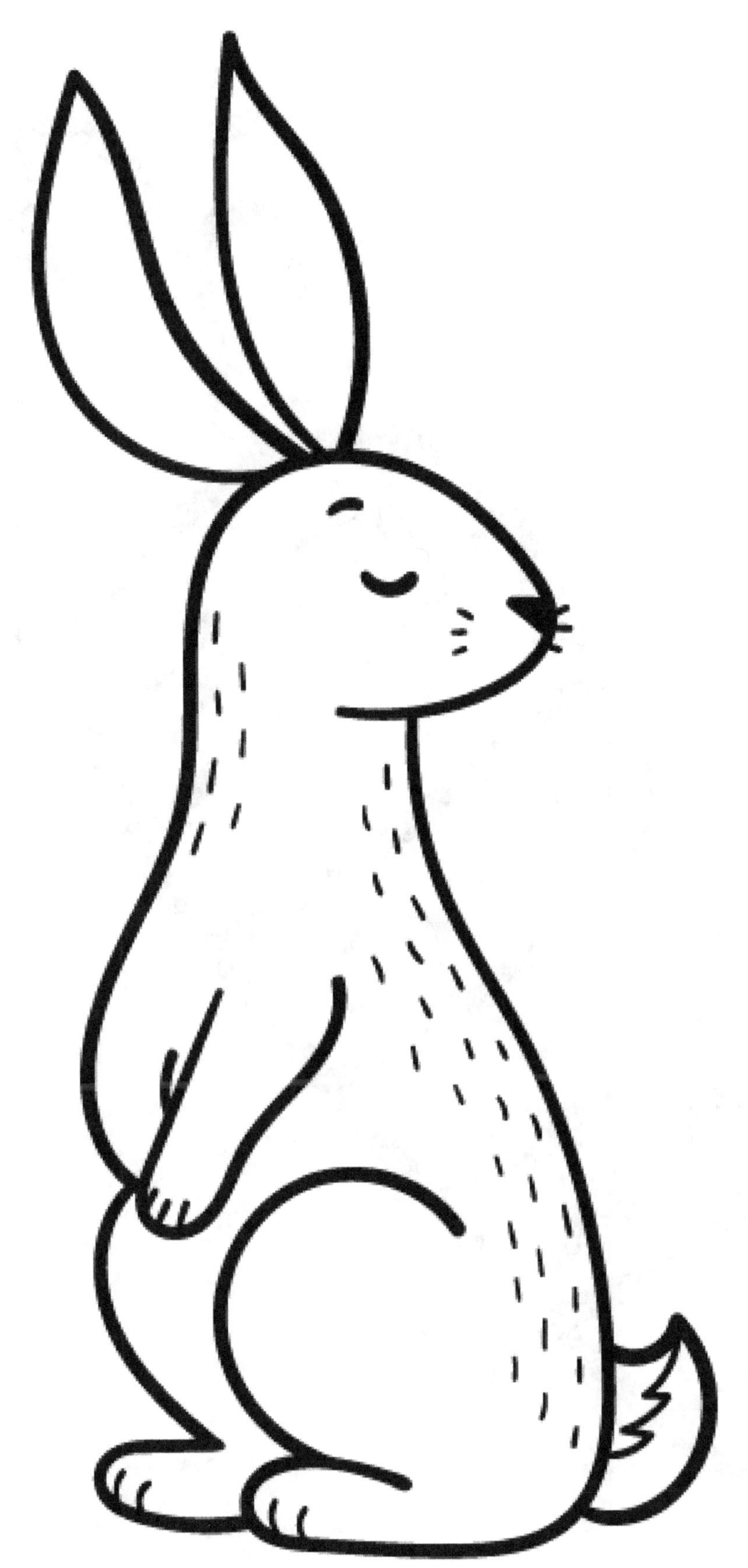

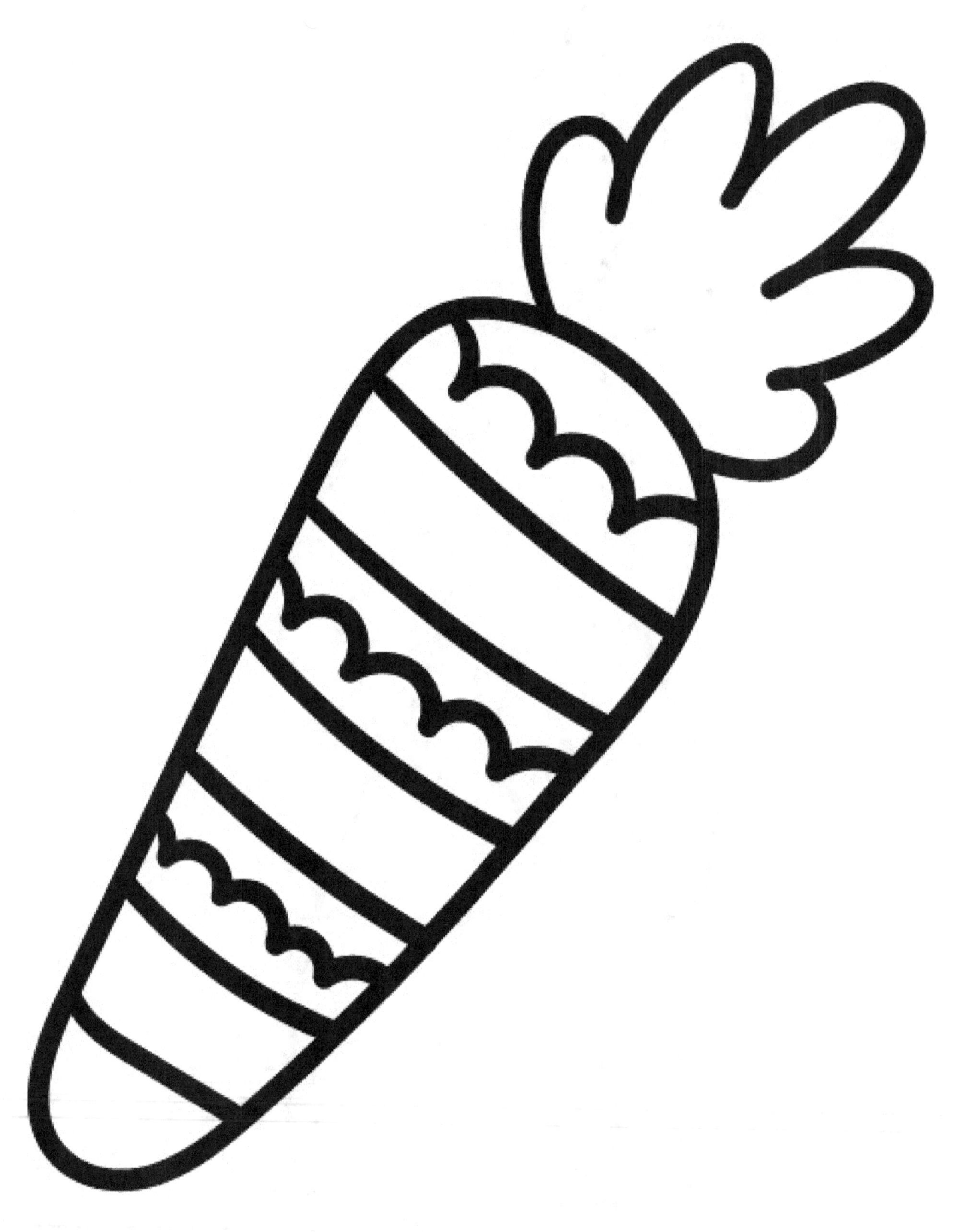

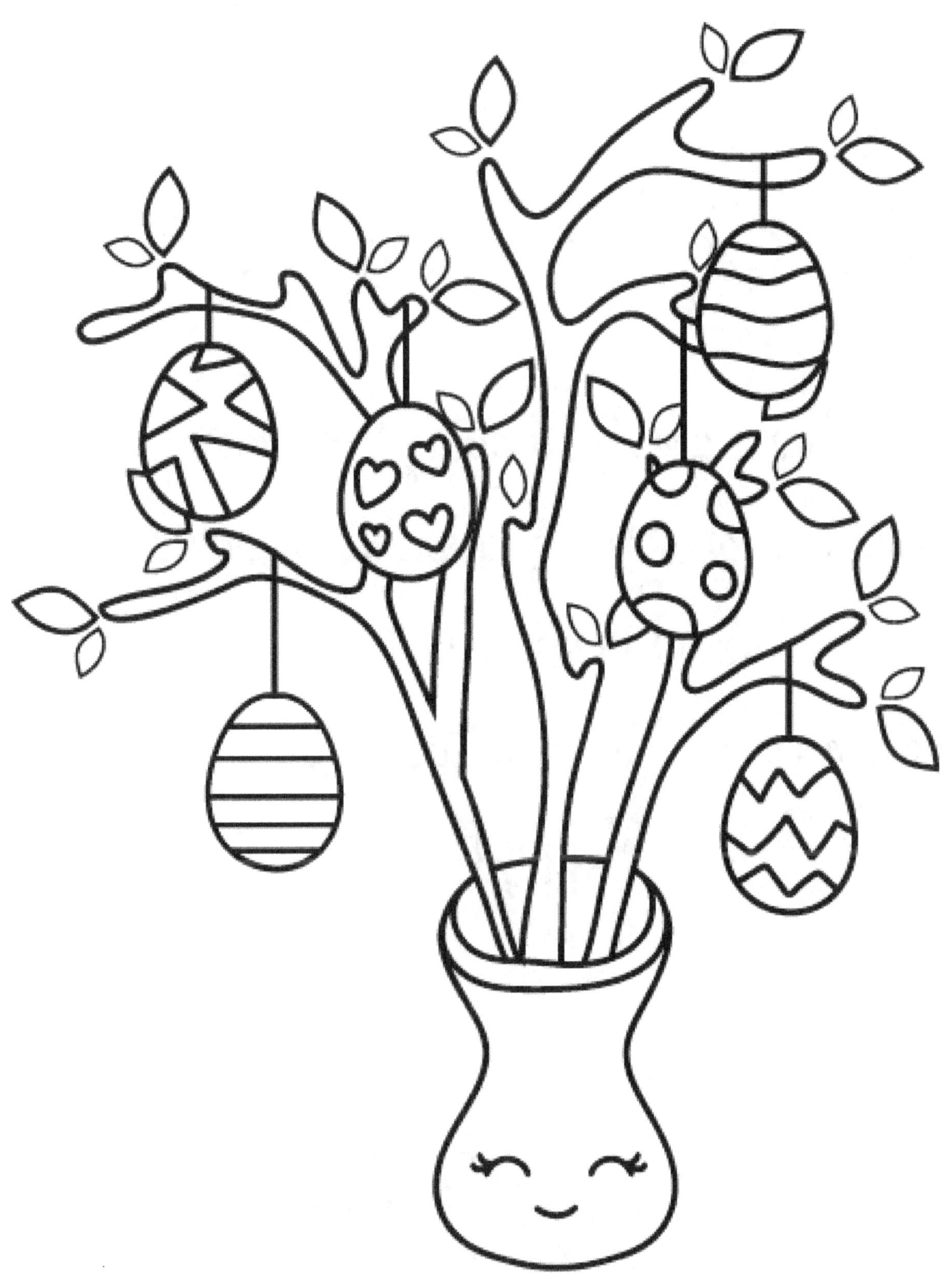

Thank you for having fun together!
We will be grateful if you share your opinion about the product with us.
For more – please visit the author's website.
Happy Easter!

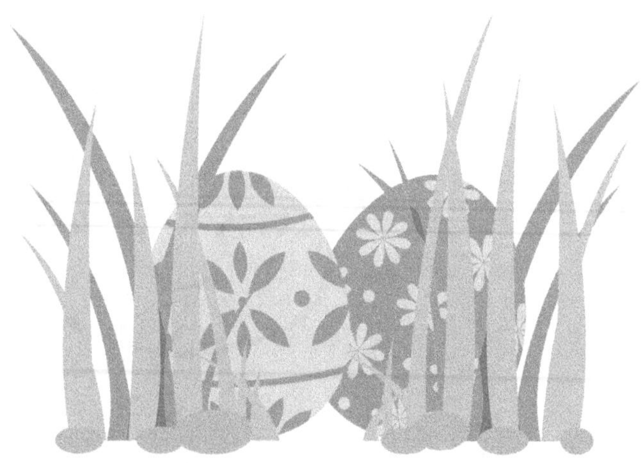